TECH MONOPOLY

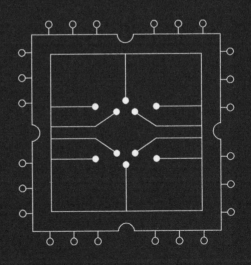

The MIT Press Essential Knowledge Series

A complete list of books in this series can be found online at
https://mitpress.mit.edu/books/series/mit-press-essential-knowledge-series.

TECH MONOPOLY

HERBERT HOVENKAMP

The MIT Press | Cambridge, Massachusetts | London, England

The MIT Press would like to thank the anonymous peer reviewers who provided comments on drafts of this book. The generous work of academic experts is essential for establishing the authority and quality of our publications. We acknowledge with gratitude the contributions of these otherwise uncredited readers.

This book was set in Chaparral Pro by New Best-set Typesetters Ltd. Printed and bound in the United States of America.

Library of Congress Cataloging-in-Publication Data

Names: Hovenkamp, Herbert, 1948– author.
Title: Tech monopoly / Herbert Hovenkamp.
Description: Cambridge, Massachusetts : The MIT Press, 2024. | Series: The MIT press essential knowledge series | Includes bibliographical references and index.
Identifiers: LCCN 2023042861 (print) | LCCN 2023042862 (ebook) | ISBN 9780262548748 (paperback) | ISBN 9780262379274 (epub) | ISBN 9780262379267 (pdf)
Subjects: LCSH: Antitrust law. | Big data. | Electronic commerce—Law and legislation. | Internet marketing—Law and legislation. | Data protection—Law and legislation.
Classification: LCC K3850 .H69 2024 (print) | LCC K3850 (ebook) | DDC 343.7307/21—dc23/eng/20231003
LC record available at https://lccn.loc.gov/2023042861
LC ebook record available at https://lccn.loc.gov/2023042862

10 9 8 7 6 5 4 3 2 1

To Maddie

CONTENTS

CONTENTS

SERIES FOREWORD

The MIT Press Essential Knowledge series offers accessible, concise, beautifully produced pocket-size books on topics of current interest. Written by leading thinkers, the books in this series deliver expert overviews of subjects that range from the cultural and the historical to the scientific and the technical.

In today's era of instant information gratification, we have ready access to opinions, rationalizations, and superficial descriptions. Much harder to come by is the foundational knowledge that informs a principled understanding of the world. Essential Knowledge books fill that need. Synthesizing specialized subject matter for nonspecialists and engaging critical topics through fundamentals, each of these compact volumes offers readers a point of access to complex ideas.

The subject of this book affects everyone, often in ways that people do not realize. Our lives are shaped by big tech. Even the vanishingly small number of people who have never used a computer or cellular phone are affected by tech products and services, including television and other media, or by family members who use them. Most Americans deal every day with at least one of the five largest tech companies, Amazon, Alphabet (formerly Google), Apple, Meta (formerly Facebook), or Microsoft. All are among the ten largest firms in the world. But the term "big tech" applies to many others, including Uber, Tesla, eBay, Samsung, Adobe, Oracle, IBM, Texas Instruments, and Intuit. Others, including Intel, Qualcomm, AMD, Micron, and TSMC (Taiwan Semiconductor), deal mainly with other business firms. Not to be forgotten are large media or social networking companies whose products are heavily digital, including Netflix, Disney, Viacom, Comcast, MSNBC, Fox, Spotify, Twitter, and TikTok. Finally are financial services firms that operate on digital platforms, including Fidelity, Schwab, PayPal, Visa, American Express, and many others.

Virtually every firm today uses tech in some way, so identifying tech firms by use is not helpful. Rather, a tech firm is one that either develops digital technology or uses it as an important part of its production or distribution.

Some firms, such as Spotify, sell digital content exclusively. Others, such as Amazon, Apple, or Texas Instruments, sell a mixture of digital and traditional "tactile" content. For example, Amazon streams music and movies but also sells toasters, bicycles, and wrenches. It will either stream you a movie or sell it to you on DVD. Others, such as Uber, sell nondigital services but operate on a digital network for coordinating rides.

The term "monopoly" almost always refers to products, not to firms. Only a few of the products sold by these firms are monopolies. Likely examples are Google Search, which controls more than 90 percent of consumer search on personal computers and mobile devices. Amazon controls nearly 70 percent of ebooks, although ebooks are only 20 percent of the overall book market. Microsoft Windows is the operating system for more than 70 percent of desktop and laptop computers, but Microsoft has a much smaller share for tablets, and its market share for smartphones is less than 1 percent. That market is dominated by Alphabet's Android and Apple's iPhone.[1] Meta (Facebook) may or may not be a dominant firm, depending on which firms are included as competitors. Netflix is very large, but it streams programming in competition with Amazon Prime, Disney+, Hulu, Apple TV, MAX (formerly HBO+), and others.

In most cases size is a poor measure of market dominance. Most firms sell multiple products. Amazon in particular sells 12 million of them. That explains why its overall size is very large, while its share of individual products is often quite small. Importantly, you as a customer are typically looking for a single product. The question for you is the number of realistically available alternatives for your search. For example, if you want to buy groceries, the fact that Amazon's grocery share is 2.5 percent gives a much better reading of the extent of the competition than does the fact that it is the largest online retailer. There may be situations in which size is more important, but one needs to be careful. In most cases market share of a particular product tells you much more about competitive alternatives than does the absolute size of the seller.

Tech markets have some features that distinguish them from "old economy" markets. For competition policy, these features pull in different directions. First, much of their output is digital. This means that the cost of selling one additional unit—such as one additional copy of an ebook or a streamed video—is very low. Second, digital output is "nonrivalrous," which means that the sale of one unit does not reduce the amount that is left over. You can stream Taylor Swift on Spotify as much as you want without reducing the amount available to others. For successful products, nonrivalrous digital output can make firms larger because there are few limits on the firms' capacity to produce more.

Third, tech firms are often organized as networks, in which firms interconnect in order to share information or intellectual property, or to engage in operations that involve many participants. One example is blanket licensing of copyrighted music. ASCAP, the American Society of Composers, Authors and Publishers, for example, has some 875,000 owner members who collectively control over 16 million digital musical works. Copyright owners grant ASCAP nonexclusive licenses, which it relicenses as a bundle to radio stations or distributors such as Spotify, which then relicense them to subscribers. Spotify alone had 489 million listeners in 2023. With blanket licensing you can subscribe to a music streaming service and have immediate access to this entire library. This market could not exist if each artist had to license her songs individually to listeners. Other networks of competitors involve the cross-licensing of patents for shared technology such as is used in cell phones or driverless cars. Still others are the "old economy" networks of teams that make up professional and amateur athletics. Ours is a world of networks, many of which are privately owned and operated. While we benefit greatly from them, they can also do anticompetitive things. For example, in 2021 the Supreme Court applied section 1 of the Sherman Antitrust Act against an agreement among NCAA colleges to limit the compensation of student athletes.[2]

"Network effects" can make networks more valuable as the number of participants is larger. For example, a dating site such as Match.com or a ride-hailing site such as

Tech firms are often organized as networks, in which firms interconnect in order to share information or intellectual property, or to engage in operations that involve many participants.

Uber becomes more attractive as it grows. As a rider, you want access to as many drivers as possible, and as a driver you are drawn to sites with more potential riders. "Indirect" network effects refer to the increased value on one side (e.g., riders) as the number on the other side (drivers) increases. The gold standard in networks is the phone system, where everyone on the system can talk to everyone else. A "dominated" network is one that is controlled by a single firm, such as Uber or the Apple operating system. But networks can also be "competitive," such as the telephone system, email system, or sports leagues in the nondigital world. These do not have a dominant firm but rather many members of various sizes. They typically act both as collaborators in the operation of the network and as competitors with one another for your business. For example, when you set up an email account you have a competitive choice among Gmail, Outlook, Yahoo, and many others. Nevertheless, these firms also collaborate to ensure interoperability.

Another feature of networks is that they are often "two-sided" markets. That means that they often obtain users and revenue from two (or more) sides. For example, a magazine, whether digital or traditional, gets revenue from both subscribers and advertisers. Too high a subscription price and it will lose readers, and then it will also lose advertisers. But too low a subscription price and it may need to sell excessive amounts of advertising to survive. As a result, it engages in "participation balancing" to find the right distribution.[3] A ride-sharing app like Uber may have to adjust its fares by the minute, with higher rush hour prices to bring in enough drivers to satisfy the number of riders and lower prices during off hours. Some two-sided markets are completely free on one side. That is true of Facebook and Google search technologies, but also of older technologies such as over-the-air radio and television.

Collectively, big tech firms have produced economic growth about three times greater than the growth rate of the economy as a whole. They have educated workforces, and produce outsize growth rates in the job market. Firms in these markets also innovate much more than the economy as a whole. Indeed, in recent years the ten firms that obtained the most patents were all tech companies. New entry into tech markets is relatively common, and even the largest tech firms appear to be competing aggressively with each other. On the buying side, consumers often have a wider variety of choices. If you are unhappy with Walmart's toaster selection you can exit the store and drive somewhere else. If you have the same experience on Amazon, you can switch with a mouse click. Information is usually more readily available on the internet, and comparison shopping is often easier. These facts lead one to wonder whether an antitrust policy of "targeting" big tech, as reflected in some journalistic writing and proposed legislation, is a good idea.

Offsetting this competition, which helps consumers, big tech firms also engage in practices that have legitimately aroused antitrust concern. They are involved in many mergers. The networks that occur so frequently in tech markets often require agreements among competitors—something that can arouse the suspicion of antitrust law enforcers.

Tech firms have also displaced many firms that were dedicated to older technologies or methods of doing business. For example, the rise of Amazon has been a brutal experience for Main Street retailers. Netflix and other video streamers have been devastating for the DVD business and traditional movie theaters. Uber and Lyft have caused serious damage to the traditional taxicab industry. The digital camera killed the film camera, and today the smartphone camera is killing the dedicated digital camera. Firms that lose out in market battles, perhaps because their business method or technology is obsolete, may continue to have influence in political institutions. To that extent the political process may lead to misguided antitrust enforcement.

Chapter 1 of this book gives an introduction to the history, capabilities, and limits of antitrust regulations. Chapter 2 discusses the problem that is sometimes characterized by the press as "bigness." Should antitrust law focus on large firms, or should it instead be concerned with high prices in consumer markets, low innovation, or harm to labor markets? Chapter 3 focuses more narrowly on the activities of technology companies themselves: What are the unique promises and threats to competition that they present? A closely related question is how much should the problems be addressed by antitrust law, or when should we turn to other areas of law, which are frequently more specific? Finally, chapter 4 examines the difficult problem of remedies. Once we have decided that Meta (Facebook) or Amazon have been behaving anticompetitively, what should we do about it? Should we break them up? If so, how? Or are there less disruptive or more effective ways of dealing with the problem? While we should condemn anticompetitive conduct, we should also hesitate to break up big tech firms without understanding the consequences.

Painting a pretty picture is not an important goal of this book. Antitrust law can be complicated and messy. It sharply divides people by politics and ideology. Some of its answers depend on assumptions that are not universally held. Producing economically and socially acceptable solutions is hard. As with so many complex policy areas, it contains a core of principles that tend to produce widespread agreement, but also some principles on both edges that are more controversial.

INTRODUCTION

The Antitrust Laws

A Thumbnail History

The United States' antitrust laws grew out of social and economic turbulence around the turn of the twentieth century. In 1890 Congress passed the Sherman Antitrust Act and President Benjamin Harrison, a Republican, signed it. The Clayton Antitrust Act was signed by President Woodrow Wilson, a Democrat, in 1914. We sometimes speak of this period as the birth of industrial America. It witnessed the dramatic rise of large firms, fueled mainly by a variety of new technologies that operated on a much larger scale than previous firms had known. Another fact was the equally dramatic rise of the labor movement, driven both by immigration and by the movement of people from rural self-employment to the factory.

American economic growth during this period was significant, but the benefits were uneven. During the late nineteenth century, the distribution of wealth became very lopsided—more than at any other time except for the present. Small entrepreneurs, farmers, and laborers were severely injured. Popular writers placed the blame squarely on large firms. In his 1901 novel *The Octopus: A Story of California*, the Progressive Frank Norris presented a fictional California railroad as an octopus, its tentacles strangling all of California's agriculture and politics. Ida Tarbell adopted that metaphor in her 1904 *History of the Standard Oil Company*. That same year *Puck*, an American humor magazine, printed its famous Standard Oil octopus cartoon entitled "Next!" The beast's tentacles extended ominously over American institutions, encircling even the Capitol (see figure 1).[1]

The octopus metaphor was brilliant. It captured not only size but also the creature's expansion beyond its core, establishing control in all places where power could be maliciously exerted. The sentient core was the octopus's body, while the mindless tentacles were its unlimited reach.

Although this rhetoric was immensely popular, no antitrust decision ever broke up a firm simply because it was big. Indeed, early antitrust decisions involving dominant firms such as Standard Oil were obsessed with anticompetitive conduct, such as buying up rivals and shutting them down, predatory pricing, exclusive contracts, secret

Figure 1

rebates, patent abuses, or excessive litigation. The law of monopoly evolved into rules that required a combination of market dominance and bad conduct.

The first section of the Sherman Antitrust Act condemned agreements "in restraint of trade," which were understood to be agreements that restricted output and thus led to higher prices. These included price fixing, but also market division agreements, which are agreements eliminating competition between firms, and boycotts. Section 1 was also the country's first merger law, applied in the 1904 *Northern Securities* case against a large railroad merger.

Section 1 does not reach the conduct of a single firm acting alone. For that, section 2 of the Sherman Antitrust

Act makes it unlawful to "monopolize" a market. Historically, a monopoly was an exclusive right granted by the government. The original British Case of Monopolies (1602) was a legal challenge to an exclusive right that Queen Elizabeth I conferred on a favored courtier to import playing cards. Another example of a government-created exclusive right was a patent or copyright. By contrast, the term "monopolize" in the Sherman Act referred to firms that dominated markets through their own conduct. That sent courts searching for business practices that could unlawfully "monopolize" a market. Congress believed that no entity should be convicted of monopolization simply because its product was better than anyone else's, but beyond that, agreement stopped. The statute also authorized the Justice Department to enforce the act, as well as private plaintiffs to sue and obtain treble damages if they succeeded.

Finally, section 8 of the Sherman Antitrust Act declared that a corporation is a single "person," creating an important dividing line between sections 1 and 2. A firm and its employees, or even a firm and its subsidiaries, are treated as one person. For example, both Google Search and the Android operating system for cellular phones are owned by Alphabet. For antitrust purposes an "agreement" among them is a unilateral act; it does not result in the formation of a cartel. In general, actions against single firms are much harder and more costly to bring than actions against cartels or collaborations.

Congress was not happy with the way the Supreme Court interpreted the Sherman Act. To be sure, it condemned price-fixing agreements, and produced big victories in 1911 against Standard Oil and American Tobacco. The court was too tolerant of patent practices, however, and it used the Sherman Act aggressively against labor strikes. There were also doubts about whether mergers were treated severely enough and whether standards for anticompetitive conduct were sufficiently clear. All three political parties in the 1912 election—Republicans, Democrats, and Theodore Roosevelt's breakaway Progressive, or "Bull Moose," Party—advocated additional antitrust legislation.

The Democrats won and responded in 1914 by enacting the wide-ranging Clayton Antitrust Act. Section 2 of that act condemned a form of predatory pricing that was believed to explain how Standard Oil had destroyed smaller rivals. Standard charged very low prices in a targeted area, financed by higher prices in areas where it already had a monopoly. Section 3 of the Clayton Act prohibited anticompetitive exclusive dealing and "tying," and specifically targeted patent practices. One practice that disturbed Congress was a patent owner's refusal to sell a patented product unless the buyer purchased some complementary product as well, thereby extending the monopoly "beyond the scope of the patent." The Supreme Court had approved such practices under the Sherman Act, refusing to condemn office equipment maker A. B. Dick for requiring purchasers of its patented copy machine to buy its unpatented ink, stencils, and paper.[2] Soon after the Clayton Act was passed the Supreme Court changed course in the *Motion Picture Patents* case, discussed below.

Section 6 of the Clayton Act was intended to immunize labor from the antitrust laws, but its exemption was interpreted very narrowly until it was further expanded during the New Deal era. Finally, section 7 of the Clayton Act contained an expanded merger provision.

Congress also passed the Federal Trade Commission (FTC) Act, which created an administrative process for antitrust enforcement and authorized the newly created FTC to pursue "unfair methods of competition." Protection of consumers was the ultimate goal, and the FTC's masthead to this day reads "Protecting America's Consumers."[3] Ever since, the civil antitrust laws have been enforced by the Justice Department's Antitrust Division and the FTC, as well as by private parties. Only the Justice Department can bring criminal actions. The FTC has the additional power to challenge practices that may not be antitrust violations but have similar effect.

Today we have a patchwork of antitrust laws passed by both the federal government and the states, which have their own antitrust laws. Federal antitrust law is the same across the country, but state rules vary from one state to another. The attorney general of each state is also authorized to bring federal antitrust actions. Today joint enforcement actions are common, brought by the federal government and as many states as wish to participate. Big antitrust actions against Microsoft, Meta, Alphabet, and Amazon have been of this kind.

The Scope of Antitrust

Economic regulation in the United States comes from many places. Utilities are regulated by federal and state agencies. Telecommunications, electronic media, and much of the internet are regulated by the Federal Communications Commission (FCC). Energy is regulated by the Federal Energy Regulatory Commission (FERC). Corporate securities, banking, and finance are regulated by their own specialized agencies.

Antitrust law is not limited to a particular industry. The antitrust laws regulate "commerce," which covers all commercial activity. This leads to some complex questions about who controls what. Answering them is beyond the scope of this book, but two points are important. The first is that antitrust law generally reaches any commercial activity unless it has been preempted by a different regulatory agency. For example, the Federal Aviation Administration preemptively regulates the licensing of aircraft and pilots, air traffic, and safety, as well as many aspects of airport operations. It does not regulate ticket pricing or airline mergers. Power over those lies with the antitrust laws. We sometimes say that antitrust law is the "residual" regulator, or the system in charge of competition beyond the reach of other regulatory provisions.

A second point is that not every economic problem is an antitrust problem. The popular press is often confused about this. Firms may have environmentally harmful practices. As a result of tax law or other policy, wealth may be concentrated in the hands of a very few. Businesses may tolerate too much discrimination or harassment among their employees. They may enable the users of their products to make untruthful political comments or suppress the political views of others. They may sell dangerous and defective products or be careless with user information. None of these things is ordinarily an antitrust issue, however. That does not mean that the legal system cannot control them, but rather that the source of control lies elsewhere.

The temptation is often strong to make antitrust law the regulator of the entire economy because the antitrust laws are very general and breathtakingly short. In two lines the first section of the Sherman Act prohibits "contracts . . . in restraint of trade." The second section prohibits those who "monopolize, or attempt to monopolize," never defining these terms. If we let our imaginations go, they can be made to cover nearly everything.

The problems with such expansive readings are manifold. First, antitrust law is complicated enough if it just

The temptation is often strong to make antitrust law the regulator of the entire economy because the antitrust laws are very general and breathtakingly short.

sticks to the historical meanings of competition and monopoly. Throwing in additional concerns, such as politics, wealth distribution, or environmental degradation, would make it less predictable and create many conflicts with other legal rules. Second, broad interpretations can easily become a way of avoiding the democratic process by getting judges to do something that Congress did not do itself. For example, someone who believes that Congress has not adequately regulated harmful water pollution may urge the courts to do it through application of the antitrust laws. But the antitrust laws never mention environmental concerns and contain no metric for evaluating them.

Another important limitation of the antitrust laws is that its concerns are fundamentally economic. Although the text of the laws is clear on this point, this has actually been a contentious issue. The basic questions are whether antitrust law should incorporate some rules about fairness, justice, or morality that might make the world a better place. One important point here is the same as was made earlier. We have other laws that are much more explicit about these issues, as well as agencies that have power over them.

What Conduct Violates the Antitrust Laws?

While antitrust law requires proof of anticompetitive conduct, the descriptions in the antitrust statutes are very general. Decades of court decisions have filled important gaps. Further, conduct is often ambiguous. It might be anticompetitive, but it might also be either harmless or beneficial. Competitors in particular are likely to make exaggerated claims about anticompetitive practices. For example, they might complain about anticompetitive standard setting when in fact they simply flunked a perfectly reasonable standard. Or they may claim predatory pricing against a rival with lower costs. On the other hand, antitrust defendants often make unsupportable claims about efficiencies or other beneficial effects of their conduct. One of antitrust law's most difficult tasks is sorting these out.

Restraints of Trade, Horizontal and Vertical

Section 1 of the Sherman Act condemns agreements "in restraint of trade." That language had a widely understood meaning prior to the antitrust laws as conduct that (1) results from an agreement and (2) reduces the volume of commercial exchange. That is largely the way we continue to use it today. Restraints that limit market output tend to drive prices higher. As fewer goods are supplied, customers bid higher prices for them.

The Sherman Act says nothing about the relationship among the parties to an agreement. Important competitive differences exist, however, between "horizontal" agreements among competitors and "vertical" agreements between sellers and buyers. Both can make the resulting entity bigger, but in different ways. Horizontal agreements instantly give the new entity a larger market share. For example, if four out of five competitors each of which has a 20 percent market share should collude, their effective share increases to 80 percent. This could give consumers fewer competitive choices. It could also enable the firms acting together to reduce market output, thereby reducing jobs, and charge a higher price or suppress wages. While a vertical agreement makes an entity bigger in the absolute sense as well, it does not result in a larger market share. If a 30 percent manufacturer and a 20 percent retailer should merge or form an exclusive agreement, their shares would still be 30 percent in manufacturing and 20 percent in retailing. The principal economic effect of vertical coordination is lower costs—a point that lawyers realized even before economists expressed it. An in-house transfer is usually cheaper than a market transaction, and the firms may coordinate their activities beneficially in other ways. The result of lower costs is higher output, which increases buying power for consumers and typically results in more jobs. To be sure, one cannot ignore the possibility that vertical integration can cause the exclusion of rivals or other harms. But the antitrust presumption is generally more favorable toward vertical as opposed to horizontal agreements.

The most troublesome horizontal agreement is price fixing, or the activity of a simple cartel whose members agree to reduce their output, leading to higher prices. Managing output is typically the most difficult part of operating a cartel. Charging a higher price is easy, but agreeing to an output reduction when the price is highly profitable is hard. Cartels often fall apart because members cheat by surreptitiously selling more than their cartel allotment. Collusion is one area of law that actually encourages cheating.

Closely related to price fixing is market division. For example, two firms that control a market may divide it into two exclusive geographic areas or customer classes: I may sell to schools and restaurants while you sell to retailers. The advantages of market division are that each firm can set its price for its own designated portion of the market. Further, cheating is often easier to detect. A cartel member may have difficulty determining whether another member is cheating on its output allotment. However, if one is assigned Pennsylvania as its territory and the other is given New Jersey, cheating sales may be easy to observe.

Concerted refusals to deal, or "boycotts," refer to various types of exclusion. Some exclusions are competitively beneficial. For example, the American Bar Association may refuse to license people who fail a bar exam, thus excluding them from the practice of law. The Supreme Court once rejected an antitrust challenge to a state bar exam.[4] Unquestionably, lawyer licensing reduces the number of people who can practice law and results in higher fees. It is justified in the belief that quality control is essential even if it is costly. Other professional rules are more suspicious. In 2015 the Supreme Court condemned a dental association's rule that only licensed dentists could professionally whiten teeth. The rule excluded dental hygienists, cosmetologists, and others who performed that service quite well but charged lower prices.[5] Several dentists had complained, not about bad outcomes, but rather about the lower prices that nondentists were charging. In this case, consumers (patients) were paying more for a rule that protected dentists from competition.

Vertical arrangements are generally less problematic. Antitrust laws can be applied to some of them, although cautiously. Franchising is one example. Baskin-Robbins, an ice cream manufacturer, might agree with a local business to create a retail ice cream outlet. The local business is an independently owned firm. The franchise agreement gives this franchisee certain rights but also some obligations. It will gain access to Baskin-Robbins's ice cream and the right to advertise itself as a Baskin-Robbins outlet, with all the customer recognition this implies. In exchange, the franchisee may promise that it will not sell any other brands of ice cream in competition with Baskin-Robbins's own. This is "exclusive dealing," which is occasionally anticompetitive. The franchisee may also promise that it will use only franchisor-provided ingredients or containers. This could be challenged as a "tying arrangement," which occurs when a seller conditions the sale of one product on the buyer's purchase of a second product.

Tying arrangements, or ties, have a checkered history in antitrust. Many of the earlier cases involved firms that sold patented products only if the buyer agreed to use the seller's own complementary products. In the 1917 Edison *Motion Pictures Patents Co.* (MPPC) case, the firm sold its film projector to theaters on the condition that the theater exhibit only MPPC's own films. Using a patented projector to monopolize the film industry might seem like an unpromising strategy, but at the time, the Edison projector was superior to its competitors. Until the Supreme Court finally condemned it, the tie shook up the entire industry. Many film producers relocated to Hollywood, California, farther away from the Edison interests.[6]

Many ties and exclusive dealing contracts, such as the ice cream franchise restrictions, are benign. Baskin-Robbins could open its own stores, but franchising is a valuable way of spreading risks and business initiative because it involves local ownership. The restrictions are necessary, however, because Baskin-Robbins is unlikely to open franchise stores just to sell other people's ice cream. The franchise system thus creates a structure that looks very much like one that is owned from top to bottom by a single firm. Since its inception in the early twentieth century, franchising has been breathtakingly successful and has served to spread business ownership widely. Franchisors are not monopolists. Even McDonald's, the largest fast food franchisor, has a market share just above 20 percent, and that is of a market limited to fast food. Baskin-Robbins has about 11 percent of a market defined as ice stream stores. Most franchises have much smaller shares.

Tying arrangements are an integral part of tech development because so many products must interact with one another. Many of these are technological ties, called tech ties, that result not from an agreement but rather from product design. For example, the modern integrated laptop computer combines many components that were once sold by separate firms and connected by wires. Alternatively, a computer program may work only with the manufacturer's own operating system. The Apple operating system for the iPhone cannot easily be made to work on non-Apple phones. Chapter 3 returns to these issues.

Monopolization
Section 2 of the Sherman Act makes it unlawful to "monopolize," but without providing any definition of that term. Many of the biggest antitrust actions against tech companies, including one in the past against Microsoft and more recent ones against Amazon, Meta (Facebook) and Alphabet (Google), are mainly monopolization cases.

When economists speak of a "monopoly," they mean a firm whose product has no competitors. They call a firm will a smaller but still large market share in a product (say, 50–70 percent) a "dominant firm." In antitrust, most of the firms called monopolists are really dominant firms. For example, monopolization actions against Microsoft, Meta, Amazon, and Alphabet all involve products whose market shares were claimed to exceed 60 percent or so, but less than 100 percent. Amazon is a very large firm, but it has nondominant market shares in most of the individual products that it sells. Critical to identifying monopolists is market definition, discussed in the next chapter.

The law of monopolization requires that a firm be "dominant" in a particular product, and also that it have committed one or more anticompetitive exclusionary practices. The emphasis on "exclusionary" is essential. Simply charging a high price is not illegal, even for a monopolist. A high price tends to bring competitors *into* a market rather than excluding them. Even so, the list of possible exclusionary practices is long. It includes "predatory pricing," which is charging a below-cost price in order to drive rivals out of business. Also included are exclusionary agreements, such as Microsoft's many threats and actions against various hardware and applications suppliers if they did not make products that worked exclusively with Microsoft's web browser at that time, Internet Explorer. These were all part of an attempt to destroy rival browser

Netscape. A single practice can be illegal, but the remedy is likely to vary as the number and range of practices is larger.

The law of monopolization also includes exclusionary misuses of intellectual property, such as enforcing improperly obtained patents. Exclusive dealing and tying arrangements acquire special significance when the firm imposing them is a monopolist. For example, Alphabet requires adopters of its Android operating system for cellular phones to make Google Search, a monopoly product, its default search engine if it wants access to the Google Play app store.

Another practice that often arises in tech is the unilateral refusal to deal, which involves a single firm's decision not to deal with someone else. The Anglo-American legal tradition has long held that freedom to select one's trading partners is central to a competitive economy. The issue comes up in a variety of situations. If Amazon decides to sell its own Amazon Basics brand of toasters or its own Kindle brand ebook readers, does it have a duty to sell the rival products of other sellers? Or if Apple opens a downtown store to sell Macs, iPads, and iPhones, does it have a duty to stock and sell Dell Computers, Android phones, or other products of competitors? These questions arise in numerous settings, in both online and offline markets. Historically there was almost never an antitrust duty. That may be changing, at least for heavily networked digital markets where cooperation is more essential to success.

One important issue in these cases is the realistic availability of alternatives. That is why they are controlled by the law of monopolization. A monopolist's refusal to carry a competitor's good may entail that the competitor will have no market access at all. But often monopoly is not threatened. For example, Amazon's share of small appliances is around 20 percent, a little less than Walmart's, and many other offline and online stores sell toasters. Should Amazon have a duty to sell a toaster for a rival who wants to sell it there? If Amazon has a duty, should it be imposed on Walmart as well? Both the suppliers' and customers' realistic range of options becomes important.

Price Discrimination

"Price discrimination" occurs when a seller makes a higher profit rate on one sale than on another. Price discrimination in and of itself is not unlawful under the antitrust laws. Indeed, most price discrimination is conducive to competition. For example, price discrimination increases output when a firm enters a new market by charging lower prices there than it charges its legacy customers. If forbidden to discriminate, it might not enter that market at all. However, antitrust law condemns such discrimination when the lower price is "predatory"—that is, below cost, but with the expectation that the seller will recoup these losses by charging monopoly prices later. Today these claims are very hard to prove, perhaps unnecessarily so.

A second form of price discrimination occurs when a supplier charges two different prices to two different dealers. In 1936 the Clayton Antitrust Act was amended by the Robinson-Patman Act (RPA) to cover such situations. Its target was A&P, a large grocery chain that was injuring many smaller, single-store grocers. The thinking of that time was that A&P had ascended to its position by forcing its suppliers to sell to it at lower prices than they were charging to smaller stores. The feared effect was that it could then undersell its rivals.

Today a broad consensus believes that the RPA was misguided. First, the chain store movement grew apace, notwithstanding the act. Customers simply wanted the lower prices and other features that larger retailers provided. Second, the act misunderstood the true reason for the rise of the chain stores, which was not discriminatory pricing but rather economies of scale and vertical integration. The chains developed their own production, warehousing, and transportation networks, providing these services for themselves more reliably and cheaply than by individual purchases in the market. As a result, the chains were able to undersell unintegrated rivals. Today the RPA is sometimes called antitrust's "wrong way Corrigan"—named after Douglas Corrigan, an aviator who filed a flight plan from Brooklyn, New York, to Long Beach, California, on a foggy night in 1938. He landed twenty-eight hours later in Dublin, Ireland.

The RPA has never been repealed, but today it is not much used. In the late 1970s the Justice Department wrote a stinging criticism of the statute, concluding that it cost $3–$6 billion annually in higher consumer prices. The Federal Trade Commission has more quietly reduced its Robinson-Patman complaints. Private enforcement remains, but the Supreme Court has been critical and has interpreted the statute very narrowly.[7] Recently the antitrust agencies have signaled plans for selective but more active enforcement.

Anticompetitive Mergers

A merger, or acquisition, occurs when one firm acquires another firm. Some mergers are stock acquisitions, in which one firm acquires all or a significant part of another corporation's shares. Others are asset acquisitions, in which one firm acquires productive assets, such as plants, from another firm. The principal competitive harm from mergers is that the post-merger firm will charge higher prices after the merger. The antitrust standards applied to mergers today are very likely too lenient. They understate the potential for higher prices. A merger may also be exclusionary, or calculated to head off small competitors before they grow into substantial rivals. This may explain acquisitions by large digital platforms, such as Facebook's purchase of Instagram.

Significant mergers must be reported to the government before they occur. The value of premerger challenge is that enjoining a merger before it occurs is much less costly than unscrambling one later, which can be likened to taking the salt back out of the soup. Better to not over-salt to begin with! One disadvantage is that assessing competitive effects is largely an exercise in predicting developments that have not yet occurred.

A merger of competitors reduces the number of firms in the market by at least one. This may increase the threat of price fixing or similar behavior. Antitrust law has had little success in prosecuting oligopoly, whereby a small number of competitors can achieve higher prices without a cartel agreement. The problem is that section 1 of the Sherman Act requires a "contract, combination, or conspiracy," which means some type of agreement among the parties. Merger enforcement is intended to prevent markets from reaching levels that enable price coordination without an express agreement.

Guidelines issued by the antitrust enforcement agencies address this problem by estimating two things: the first is how "concentrated" a market will be after a merger occurs, and the second is how much the merger in question will increase concentration. The first task is to define the market carefully. Then the agencies compute the market share of each firm and apply a "concentration index" that varies with the number of firms in the market and their size variations.

Real-world mergers are almost always more complex than this description suggests. Typically, the firms' products are differentiated. For example, consider a merger between Microsoft and Apple. Both make computer operating systems, but they are quite different and operate on different computers. If our market definition places them into the same market, we end up treating them as perfect competitors. By contrast, if our market definition includes only one, then we treat the two firms as if they do not compete at all. Neither answer is accurate.

A second method of evaluating mergers is more mathematical but also more precise. It is also more data-intensive and thus cannot be applied in every situation. Briefly, the method assumes that a merger between two "close" competitors in a differentiated market creates a greater danger of a price increase than a merger between two firms that are more remote. While quite technical, this method does not require a market definition. One of its advantages is that it provides a "direct" measure of a merger's ability to cause a price increase, rather than simply inferring it from a high market share.[8] Because it is so data dependent it tends to work well on internet markets, where nearly all transactions are recorded.

Antitrust challenges to mergers involving newly emergent, or "nascent," competitors is not as well established today as it should be. That may be in the process of changing.

At this writing mergers involving potential rather than actual competitors have received increased attention.

Antitrust and Economics

The antitrust laws use economic language, and not subtly. All of the Sherman Act and Clayton Act prohibitions are expressed in terms such as "restrain trade," "monopolize," or "substantially lessen competition." The application of applied economics to antitrust as it is done today is largely the invention of the Progressives, mainly from 1900 through the early 1930s.[9] In very general terms, economists make two kinds of contributions. First, at the academic level, economists are responsible for much of the economic theory that forms the basic structure of antitrust law. This occurs mainly through the economic disciplines of price theory and industrial organization. Both of these are concerned with microeconomics, which means that they focus on the operation of individual markets.

The field of macroeconomics, which is concerned with the economy as a whole, has very little role in antitrust. This fact seems surprising to some and unfortunate to others. After all, should not antitrust be concerned with such things as the general rate of economic growth, inflation, or the overall health of the labor market? The answer is yes, but only to the extent that healthy and competitive

The antitrust laws use economic language, and not subtly. All of the Sherman and Clayton Act prohibitions are expressed in terms such as "restrain trade," "monopolize," or "substantially lessen competition."

markets for specific products are important foundations for a healthy economy overall. The issue will come up once or twice in this book but not often, and macroeconomics is almost never relevant to specific antitrust cases.

The second way that economics comes into antitrust is through expert consulting and testimony. Economists give firms and agencies antitrust advice, and also serve as expert witnesses. The role of economic experts is similar to their role in other types of complex litigation. They help determine whether the basic economic conditions for an antitrust violation are present, whether there is evidence of causation and injury in private cases, and the measure of damages. The use of economists in this fashion is not controversial, although specific methods may be. Most of the economics that is applied in antitrust today is neither high theory nor cutting edge. One of its most valuable uses is to prevent people from making dumb mistakes.

Should antitrust policy go further and consider "noneconomic" factors, such as political power, fairness, labor relations, or climate change as important goals? Over the years many writers have toyed with this issue, but courts rarely oblige. Without answering this question decisively, there are good reasons not to range too far beyond economics.

First, as noted above, is the language of the antitrust statutes. Debates about whether antitrust should have a significant noneconomic content were already prominent when both the Sherman Act and the Clayton Act were passed. Some members of Congress and presidential candidates such as William Jennings Bryan argued for injecting more concerns about morality into antitrust. None of the antitrust laws themselves reflects it. Even the major Progressive expansion of antitrust law in the Clayton Act of 1914 condemned practices only when they threatened to "substantially lessen competition" or "tend to create a monopoly." The term "unfair methods of competition" was included in the Federal Trade Commission Act, which can be enforced only by the FTC itself. That agency maintains a Consumer Protection division, which has the power to control things like false and misleading business statements when no threat of monopoly is present. But that is largely where it ends. Beyond that, the text of the antitrust laws provides no reason for including noneconomic factors.

Second, a limitation to economics is necessary to avoid turning the antitrust laws into a kind of judicial imperialism. The antitrust laws were never intended to rule the policy world, or even all of the economic world. We already have plenty of policies governing the distribution of wealth, political expression, business torts, employment discrimination, and climate change. As frustrated as people may be with Congress's failure to act in certain areas, that is no reason to use the antitrust laws to hijack the democratic process.

Third is the problem of stability and management. Antitrust is difficult enough for courts to handle under an economic approach. Inclusion of noneconomic factors could make it far more difficult. For example, a large firm may benefit consumers and labor by offering lower prices that rivals cannot match. As output increases in response to lower prices, the demand for jobs goes up. Assuming that this firm has not done anything else that could be construed as anticompetitive, should we create an offsetting "fairness" rule that finds an antitrust violation simply to protect smaller competitors? Doing so would necessarily involve trading off the welfare of consumers and labor against that of the smaller competitors.

Ignoring consumers and labor was a serious error that Congress made in passing the Robinson-Patman Act in the 1930s. Congress listened to small-business interest groups that wanted protection for traditional single-store sellers. Meanwhile, customers were voting with their feet and contributing to the meteoric rise of large retailers. To be sure, firms often grow large by engaging in anticompetitive practices, but then a court should identify those practices and determine a remedy that is targeted to them.

The Principal Schools of Antitrust Thought

For nearly a century, antitrust policy has been dominated by two schools of thinking about competition policy, the Harvard school and the Chicago school. A diverse and loosely affiliated group that has emerged more recently on the political left styles itself "neo-Brandeisian."

The Harvard school originated in the 1930s and was heavily focused on market power, which is the subject of the next chapter. One characteristic was its belief that markets differ from one another. The problem areas were not traditional commodities such as grain but rather manufactured products, characterized by larger firms, fewer producers in a market, and more variation among them. The result in those markets could be higher prices. The Harvard school was also concerned with barriers to entry, or the reasons why new firms were able to come into some markets less readily than others. Economists' traditional concern about monopoly had been tempered by their faith that new firms would always enter if existing firms raised their prices unreasonably. But in some industries that did not appear to happen. One problem was a proliferation of patents. Another was production technologies that required large firms. Yet another was "exclusionary" practices such as predatory pricing or tying arrangements that gave large advantages to firms that were already in the market.

The result of this thinking at mid-century was decisions that emphasized market structure but deemphasized anticompetitive conduct. According to the emergent "structure-conduct-performance" (S-C-P) paradigm, non-competitive market structures led naturally to harmful conduct. This in turn led to poor performance, expressed in higher prices, lower output, or less innovation. Under entailment rules of logic, if S entails C and C entails P, then C drops out as an important variable. So the most extreme statements of structuralism were that the best way to control monopoly was to look exclusively at structure. No court or legislation ever went that far, but a movement for "no fault" monopoly took hold. Its promoters believed that the government should identify industries that had durable dominant firms and break them up, thus creating more competition. In 1972 Senator Philip A. Hart of Michigan proposed a concentrated industries act, which would have broken up firms in industries with a small number of competitors, such as the automobile industry. The legislation never passed.

In hindsight, the Harvard structuralist school had many important things to say, and it was right to focus on problematic industries. For example, only relatively large firms can produce automobiles or aircraft. We are less concerned about French restaurants or landscapers. The Harvard school did bring an end to a certain naïveté about patents that saw them as invariably good things. In fact, we issue too many patents, often for trivial inventions, and excessive patenting makes industries less responsive to competitive pressure.

Patents actually operate very differently in different industries. At one extreme is machinery and chemicals, including pharmaceuticals, where they can be very valuable. At the other extreme is information technologies such as computers, the internet, and telecommunications, where they are often little more than costly nuisances. This differential treatment was quite consistent with the Harvard approach of seeing different effects in different markets. A great deal of patenting in internet markets falls into the latter category.

The Chicago school emerged in the 1940s as a neoliberal reaction to the New Deal.[10] Its promoters emphasized a return to older economic principles that minimized differences among markets. They also believed that the concerns with market concentration and entry barriers were heavily exaggerated. The Chicago school was heavily influenced by positivistic science, which urged rejection of ideas that could not be empirically tested.

The Chicago school advised much less intervention in markets. It believed that concentrated industries and large firms were necessary to create low-cost production and incentivize innovation. It criticized the Harvard school for being overly preoccupied with tying arrangements and other vertical restraints. Finally, it was much more enthusiastic about patents.

The Chicago school's distrust of theories of imperfect competition was partly undermined by empirical work in the 1970s and 1980s. Today, imperfect-competition models dominate most economic thinking. Accordingly, antitrust law is more supportive of active enforcement than the adherents of the Chicago school were, and more consistent with the Harvard school. There also seems to be little doubt that markets do, in fact, differ significantly from one another. Some are more prone to noncompetitive outcomes than others. Finally, the Chicago school's strong claims about efficiencies have not held up well empirically—a particular problem for a theory that emphasized testability and empirical research.

While both the Harvard and Chicago schools contributed a great deal to antitrust thinking, both went to extremes, and today we have pulled back from both. Antitrust remains a discipline driven by economic theory, coupled with a need for serious fact finding. That leads to one important criticism of antitrust, which is that it is too costly. Legislation that provides one-size-fits-all rules simply cannot take market differences into account, but individual rule making is fact intensive and expensive.

At odds with the Harvard and Chicago schools are the neo-Brandeisians, named after Justice Louis D. Brandeis, an opponent of "bigness" in business. Prominent characteristics of neo-Brandeisian antitrust thinking are its opposition to large firms and to tech, its favoritism toward small business, and its indifference toward consumers, even wishing to condemn mergers because they result in lower prices. The movement is particularly agitated about large digital platforms such as Alphabet (Google), Amazon,

Apple, and Meta (Facebook), as well as other tech firms that have displaced older technologies, such as Uber. For example, while Walmart is about the same size as Amazon and engages in many similar practices, it receives much less scrutiny. Because of the neo-Brandeisian antitech bias and small firm protectionism, the firms that it tends to dislike are also ones that consumers like.

The neo-Brandeisian movement is strongly populist. It is often contemptuous of expertise, particularly in the economic realm. One of its characteristics is nostalgia for a world of small entrepreneurs and simpler technologies and distribution.[11] While some of its criticisms are interesting, others seem not to be well thought out. For example, neo-Brandeisians often call for big tech to be broken up, without providing detail about how this should be done or who would be affected by it. Its severe critiques of high product output as an antitrust goal are in conflict with its protective attitude toward labor. The neo-Brandeisian obsession with bigness disregards the fact that large firms often have lower prices, do disproportionately more innovation, and generally pay higher wages than small firms. To be sure, large firms may wield significant political power, but trade associations made up of smaller firms have historically had much more success in lobbying Congress or state legislatures, and also have engaged in more cartel-like anticompetitive activities.[12] For example, Brandeis was a champion of the small business war on the chain stores, such as A&P, that were beginning to dot the landscape in the 1920s and 1930s. They drove many single-store operators out of business. But consumer preferences were too strong. The chain stores won that battle and today are an accepted and highly competitive institution in American economic life. Neo-Brandeisian proposals often recall a warning from Judge Learned Hand many years ago: the "successful competitor, having been urged to compete, must not be turned upon when he wins."[13] His quick characterization may seem unfair. At this writing perhaps it is, because few neo-Brandeisian policies have yet been implemented. Chapters 3 and 4 return to these issues.

Conclusion: The Goals of the Antitrust Laws

Every area of law is obsessed with ultimate goals. For example, criminal law contains a never-ending debate about whether its goal should be punishment of wrongdoers or deterrence. Tort law has a similar dialogue about whether it should minimize the social cost of accidents or punish careless behavior. Should the goal of medical malpractice law be compensation of victims or deterrence of negligent professional conduct? A statement of goals can be very important for expressing a legal area's fundamental concerns. Nevertheless, in most areas the legal system sputters along without drawing any final conclusions about goals.

One principle that is frequently stated today is that antitrust policy should seek to protect the competitive process. Stated as a slogan, that sounds attractive and is hard to dispute. One problem, however, is that the term "competitive process" has no content. As a result, judges who have very different views about policy and outcomes articulate it as an antitrust goal.[14] It's a little like saying that the purpose of economics is to support free markets or that the goal of the legal system is to do justice.

For a half century, antitrust policy has been guided by something called the "consumer welfare" principle. As a slogan, "consumer welfare" is also hard to dispute. It can also mean multiple inconsistent things. The Chicago school, led by Robert Bork in the 1970s, adopted a cynical version of consumer welfare that included producer profits as part of the welfare of consumers. The argument was that, under competition, producer profits will be competed into rewards for consumers. Whether that was true or not, the Borkean revolution in the 1980s coincided with a massive increase in producer profits, a severe decline in the fortunes of labor, and very likely higher prices for consumers. An underdeterrent antitrust law was certainly not the only contributor to these changes, but it did its part.

By contrast, what is sometimes called the "true" consumer welfare principle looks exclusively at the welfare of consumers. In general, they are better off when market output and innovation are higher and prices are lower.

One of its values is that it provides an actual target for measurement. While "output" and "price" are not always easy to measure, particularly if output includes innovation, they are nevertheless meaningful, measurable concepts.

One critique of this principle is that a goal of high output and low prices disfavors higher-cost firms, which are typically older, smaller, and often use older technologies or methods of distribution. The simple fact is that the act of stating a meaningful goal requires some choosing of sides. This version of the consumer welfare principle generally sides with consumers and labor, both of which benefit from lower prices and higher output. It is less protective of firms that have higher costs or that do less innovation. This is one place where a little bit of macroeconomics can sneak in. As individual markets are more competitive and produce more, the economy as a whole does better as well.

ANTITRUST AND POWER

Market Power

Antitrust is concerned with market power, which is a firm's power to profit by raising prices above cost. One result of monopoly is that consumers pay too much. Another is that the output reduction that accompanies monopoly reduces the number of jobs. A monopolistic price increase that reduces product demand by, say, 20 percent, will very likely reduce jobs by about that amount. Consumers and workers both benefit from competitive markets.

To exercise market power, a firm must be able to reduce the output of the entire market, not just its own. Under perfect competition a firm charges a price equal to its immediate ("marginal") cost. As competition becomes less perfect, the firm's price rises above its costs. It reaches its highest level when the firm is a monopolist, or the only

One result of monopoly is that consumers pay too much. Another is that the output reduction that accompanies monopoly reduces the number of jobs.

firm in its market. Cartels cause the same problem. In fact, a perfectly functioning cartel charges the same price as a dominant firm with the same market share. As a result, the question of market power is universal, in the sense that it applies to all types of antitrust practices, including mergers, joint ventures, and other agreements. The fundamental question is whether the challenged practice gives a firm, a cartel, or other group the power to reduce market output and raise its prices above cost. If so, consumers and labor will suffer.

A firm's market power is limited by two things. First, as a firm charges higher prices, customers try to abandon it for a different product or supplier. If too many customers do this, the firm's high price will be unprofitable. On the other side, when a firm raises its prices, competitors will be motivated to substitute *into* that firm's market. For example, if a restaurant increases its pizza prices, competing restaurants will be tempted to add pizza to their menu in order to capitalize on these higher returns. The new competition will push prices back down.

The *American Can* case is a cautionary tale of what can happen when a firm has an exaggerated belief about its market power. Early in the twentieth century, American Can's CEO, Edwin Norton, attempted to create a monopoly in metal cans for preserving food. Cans had been made by hand in small shops by skilled artisans, but Norton both developed and acquired mechanized equipment capable of cutting, forming, and soldering cans in high volume. He also bought several old can-making companies and shut them down. He entered into exclusive contracts with many makers of the new machinery and attempted to tie up the market for tin plate with exclusive agreements. Within a few years Norton believed he had acquired a monopoly and significantly increased his can prices. Almost immediately dozens of new firms emerged. They reentered the market with any equipment they could find in "old lumber rooms," as the court put it. American Can's market share went into free fall. Norton attempted to solve the problem in the worst possible way—by buying up competitors' cans and throwing them away. Of course, that induced even more firms to enter can production. By the time the case was decided, American Can's market share had fallen to 50 percent and was still in decline.

This history of movements in response to price changes provides a useful definition of market power: Market power is the ability to profit from above-cost prices without inducing so many losses from customer defection or competitor expansion that the price increase must be reversed. Market power is easy to specify mathematically but difficult to measure empirically. Courts have developed a shortcut, which is to define a "relevant market" of goods that are close substitutes for one another and then calculate the defendant's "market share," which is a ratio of a firm's own output to that of the entire market. For example, if the market produces 1,000 identical units, a firm that produces 200 units has a 20 percent market share. Higher market shares create an inference of greater market power.

The relevant market is not strictly an antitrust invention. A version of it was well established in microeconomics under the imposing name of "partial equilibrium analysis." If a market is properly defined, the goods inside the market compete with one another for a customer's purchase, but do not compete with goods outside the market. That concept is clear enough, but the real world is a messier place. For example, there is very likely a market for tea, which means that different producers of tea compete with one another for sales. Tea in this conception does not compete with coffee, water, milk, or other beverages. Strictly speaking, that is not true. For example, a disastrous tea crop and high prices may induce some people to switch to coffee or another beverage.

As you might guess, antitrust litigation includes countless disputes about what does and does not go into a market. Antitrust decisions have concluded that cans and bottles are in the same market; that cellophane by itself does not constitute a market, for said market also includes tin foil and wax paper; that the market for social networking may include Facebook and Instagram but not Twitter (now X) or TikTok.[1] Most markets for manufactured goods, and tech markets in particular, are prone to

Market power is the ability to profit from above-cost prices without inducing so many losses from customer defection or competitor expansion that the price increase must be reversed.

"product differentiation." That means that firms produce competing but distinguishable products, such as Windows and Mac computers, iPhones and Android phones, Netflix and MAX, Facebook and X. The list goes on. These products compete on features as much as price. On the consumer end, products that are free to users, such as Facebook, X, and Gmail, compete entirely on features.

Relevant markets in antitrust are frequently measured by a "hypothetical monopolist" test, which asks what is the *smallest* set of sales for which a firm could be a monopolist. The test requires some economics, but it gives good results when the data are available. Suppose that ten firms produce similar but not identical products. For example, they may produce a variety of wrapping materials, such as cellophane, wax paper, glassine, brown wrapping paper, metal foil, paper boxes, and so on. We want to know whether cellophane enjoys significant market power. First we examine pricing and substitution among these products. We might observe that when the cellophane price increases, many customers switch to wax paper, a small number switch to foil, and even fewer switch to cardboard boxes. A "close" substitute must be included in the market, or the intending monopolist that increases its price will lose too many sales. How close is close depends on the rate of substitution, which can be measured if the data are available. As each close substitute is placed in the market, however, the market share of the defendant declines. For example, if the relevant market was "cellophane," DuPont, which held a controlling patent, might control 100 percent of it. But if the market includes wax paper, DuPont's share of the combined market might drop to 20 percent, insofar as wax paper was much more widely used in the 1950s when the *DuPont* case was decided. Adding in foils would cause the market share to drop even further.

Sometimes the price and switching information needed for the hypothetical monopolist test is not available. Then the courts look to poorer alternatives, such as usage in the industry, physical characteristics, the way that the trade literature groups certain products, and the like. These methods are generally less reliable.

Someone who has market power does not necessarily have it everywhere. Large tech platforms such as Meta (Facebook) operate in world markets. By contrast, while Uber operates worldwide, its market share differs from one city to another. In some cities, such as Copenhagen, it does not operate at all. Yet other firms, such as Zoe's Computer Repair, might operate in only one city. In addition to the product market, antitrust courts must identify a "geographic market" in which the firm has market power. The methods for measuring geographic and product markets are essentially the same. If Zoe's Computer Repair raises prices in Miami, customers might respond by driving farther to get their computers fixed. Alternatively, technically trained people might see the higher prices as an opportunity to open a computer repair shop in Miami. A full description of a firm's market must include both a product definition and a geographic definition. In the case of Uber that might be something like "customer-hailed rides in Philadelphia."[2]

Market power refers both to the power of a single firm acting alone and of a group of firms acting together. We fear cartels because, while each individual firm may lack power to raise prices, if all or most of them conspire, they can succeed. Equally worrying is the fact that the formation of a cartel can create market power almost instantly, sometimes with a single meeting. By contrast, the creation of single-firm power can take years or decades of innovation, predation, and sometimes good luck.

We sometimes estimate the market power of a group by adding up their individual shares. That only works for competitors, or firms that sell in the same market. Networks often include participants that are not only competitors but also those that are vertically related or sell complementary products. Vertical and complementary agreements (such as between a hardware provider and a software firm) do not ordinarily increase anyone's market share. They may create anticompetitive threats among firms that already have market power, however, particularly if they deal with each other exclusively. For example, the *Microsoft* antitrust remedy prohibited exclusive agreements requiring various applications producers to favor

Internet Explorer, its internet browser. The fear was that, given Windows' dominant share, an exclusive agreement could effectively create dominance in the browser market as well.

Some firms sell groups of products that do not compete with one another but seem sufficiently integrated together to be placed in the same market. For example, a hospital might offer surgical services, obstetrics, internal medicine, and urology, to name just a few. Someone in need of a colonoscopy cannot substitute cranial surgery, so why place them into a single "market"? This issue has particular currency for large digital platforms, many of which offer several noncompeting goods and services. For example, the FTC's complaint against Meta alleged that Facebook was monopolizing a market for "personal social networking services." That market consists of messaging, timeline posting, photo and video posting, social network formation, and the like. Further, other firms offer a subset of these services. For example, YouTube posts videos but does not do many of the other things that Facebook does.

These aggregated but noncompeting products are called "cluster" markets. Such markets make sense when (1) it is cheaper for the services to be supplied together or customers want the group of products aggregated in one place, *and* (2) duplication of the entire grouping is difficult. Hospitals are a good example. Patients typically do not value more than one or two of the hospital's services at a time; however, the hospital can save substantial resources by delivering them from a single facility and the patient must obtain them at a hospital. In digital markets, Facebook offers a combination of services that users can select on demand when they need one, and it is also more efficient for Facebook to offer them together on a common platform.

Even if we permit cluster markets, we must make sure that the cluster story fits the antitrust problem at hand. For example, if we are concerned about Amazon's ability to charge monopoly prices for groceries, it does not make much sense to start out with Amazon's overall position in internet sales. For the customer looking for groceries, Amazon's 2.5 percent market share in grocery sales seems decisive. Further, customers do not need a store of Amazon's magnitude to buy groceries. It is not likely to get away with a monopoly price increase. The fact that it dominates ebook sales or has a much larger share of electric toasters won't make much difference. By contrast, if Amazon proposed to merge with eBay, then a look at overall sales in products where the two compete would be important.

Economists have also made enormous progress in the "direct" measurement of market power. Direct measurement uses econometrics to assess a firm's power to charge prices above its costs. It does this not by defining a market but rather by looking at how a firm's sales respond to price changes.[3] Although direct measurement of market power is more accurate, it is also more technical and has met resistance from some judges who have been trained in the traditional tools of market definition. The antitrust enforcement agencies, which have staffs of able economists, generally do not share this reluctance. Within them the popularity of direct, more economic methods of measuring power has increased significantly.

A few decisions have also found market power based on "lock-in," or the specific costs of substitution in "aftermarkets." These are markets for some good or service that complements a product that the customer already owns, such as repair parts or higher levels of a game. In the Supreme Court's *Kodak* decision, Kodak had a market share of less than 25 percent of high-speed photocopiers. But the plaintiffs successfully argued that someone who *already owned* a Kodak copier was "locked in" and could use only repair parts compatible with Kodak's equipment. For some of the patented parts, Kodak was the only one that made and sold them. The court rejected the argument that a "rational" customer would never have bought the copier to begin with if she had known that the price of repair parts was so high.[4] If read too broadly, *Kodak* threatens to turn many quite competitive firms into monopolists. At the same time, it states an important point. For example, by insisting that iPhone owners purchase only through its App Store, Apple may be able to charge higher prices for apps even if it is not a monopolist in the phone market. We will return to this issue in our discussion of switching costs.

Power, or Size?

Market power is not the same thing as large size, or "bigness." Consider the only swimming pool contractor in Ozona, Texas, an isolated town with fewer than 3,000 people. That contractor may have five employees and install a dozen pools annually. Yet it may be able to charge a price higher than its costs because customers in Ozona do not have good alternatives. By contrast, Chrysler owns multiple plants with nearly 90,000 employees in the United States alone. It has less market power, however, because it competes intensely with GM, Ford, Toyota, and other carmakers. Historically the term "monopoly" referred to companies that had exclusive control over a product, without regard to size. Many, such as patentees or the owner of a toll bridge with an exclusive grant, were quite small.

Market power is universally regarded by the courts as the correct measure of antitrust monopoly. The popular literature is sometimes mistaken about this. In fact, whether we select size or market power as antitrust's target depends on our purpose. If the goal is to protect smaller competitors from the lower costs and (typically) greater innovation of larger firms, then size is relevant.

A larger firm can often injure a smaller rival even if the larger firm has only a small percentage of the market. For example, the chain grocer A&P drove several small grocers out of business in the 1920s and 1930s even though it did not have a dominant market share. While Amazon is a very large firm, for most products its market share is not more than 15 percent or 20 percent, and for groceries it is under 3 percent. The reason is that Amazon's sales are distributed over some 12 million products, and customers are typically looking for only one or a few. So *their* choices are dictated by Amazon's market share in the particular product they want, not by Amazon's overall size.

On the other hand, if the antitrust goal is to protect consumers by providing low prices and labor by facilitating high output, then market share is the relevant measure. A low cost firm with a small market share can easily undersell higher cost rivals. What it cannot do, however, is force overall market prices to be higher or wages lower. For that a firm needs to have a sufficiently large share to prevent rivals from being more competitive. With a 20 percent share of the market for kitchen toasters, Amazon may very well be able to undersell smaller rivals. But it would not have the power to compel higher marketwide prices. If Amazon's market share were 80 percent, however, that could be entirely different.

Many large firms have lower costs than small firms operating in the same market. They typically pay higher wages and have better-developed systems of employee benefits. The innovation story is more complex. The rate of innovation is lowest at the two extremes of pure monopoly and severe competition among tiny firms. Most innovation is done in the middle, in moderately concentrated markets by firms of various sizes. Particularly in tech, however, some small firms are highly innovative.[5]

One issue that is sometimes confused with bigness is a firm's ability to leverage power in one market into a second market. We consider this claim further in the following chapter's discussion of "abuse" of a dominant position. Alphabet has been accused of this. It makes the market-dominant Google search engine the default choice on phones that use the Android operating system, which it also owns. Here, however, the issue is not bigness but rather the fact that a firm operating in two (or more) markets may be able to use its position in one market to affect a second market. Even a fairly small firm that operates in two markets could do that. While the idea has been overused it is hardly fanciful, provided it is limited to practices that cause real competitive harm.

Often what is treated as undesirable multimarket leveraging is nothing more than cost savings. For example, a small firm that operates both a dairy and a vegetable farm might reduce its costs by delivering both products to grocers in the same truck. A firm that produced only one of these products could not do that. Or a multiproduct firm

such as Amazon might save costs by using the same platform, warehouses, and billing across multiple products.
But it is not the purpose of the antitrust laws to prevent
firms from finding ways to lower their costs. Accordingly,
we should be suspicious of legislation that prevented
someone from delivering dairy and vegetable products
from the same truck. It is most likely instigated by single-
product sellers in order to destroy the advantages of selling two products together.

Technology can play a role in issues about market
power or size. For example, small firms are injured when
they are unable to adapt new technologies or innovations
in distribution. When they can do so, small firms do quite
well. In general, both consumers and labor benefit from
higher output, better quality, and more innovation. Enabling those outcomes should be the goal of antitrust
policy, without regard to whether we are protecting small
or large firms. One problem is the relationship between
mergers and innovation. While the evidence is mixed, it
suggests that on balance, mergers reduce the incentives
to innovate, although that effect shows up more in some
markets than others.[6]

One additional objection to large firms is that they
have more political power. The argument has frequently
been aimed at big tech. Historically, however, more anticompetitive business political influence has come from
trade associations.[7] These are typically made up of smaller

firms. For example, the National Retail Druggists' Association (NARD) was an organization of small druggists that used its lobbying power in the 1920s and 1930s to legislate "fair trade," which forced larger, lower-cost druggists to charge higher prices. The Robinson-Patman Act was championed in the 1930s by the United States Wholesale Grocers Association, an organization of small grocers that organized against the rise of the "chain store." Today that mantle has been picked up once again by the National Grocers Association, which wants to guarantee small grocers higher retail prices.[8] Associations of car dealers have persuaded many states to combat Tesla by prohibiting "direct" sales of automobiles, thus eliminating car dealers, even if customers prefer direct buying. In Oregon and New Jersey, the Gasoline Retailers Association was able to obtain statewide prohibitions on self-service gasoline, targeting gasoline sales by convenience stores. In one important decision the Supreme Court condemned a policy supported by the North Carolina Dental Association that forbade nondentists from whitening teeth.[9] The historical record of trade associations obtaining legislative favors to protect smaller firms' higher prices or less innovative methods is far more disturbing than the history of legislation obtained by large techs.

A popular concern is sometimes stated that the purpose of antitrust is to "level the playing field." That can mean many things. For example, it may refer to preventing large firms from engaging in anticompetitive practices, which good antitrust policy should do. But it should not be interpreted to mean that antitrust law should hobble larger firms by raising their costs or limiting their ability to innovate, simply for the protection of small firms. In the business world a level playing field frequently does not exist. Automobile and microprocessor production will always favor large firms, and highly innovative firms will usually outrun those who are less creative.

A related concern is the migration of the retail economy from Main Street to cyberspace. That migration has clearly injured traditional brick-and-mortar retailers. But that leaves two questions. First, is this a problem that requires government intervention? And second, is antitrust law the way to go about it?

If Main Street requires assistance, it should take the form of support for the displaced, not suppression of the innovators. The history of innovation policy is strewn with the corpses of firms that either resisted it or were unable to keep up. The automobile put countless blacksmiths and carriage makers out of business. The electronic calculator killed the slide rule, and digital photography bankrupted both very large Kodak and thousands of small film developers. The rise of music and video streaming has severely harmed the markets for physical CDs, DVDs, and even movie theaters. This is only a few of the many times that more innovative or technologically advanced companies ruined less nimble competitors. It should not be antitrust's role to protect them by suppressing innovation.

The Supreme Court lost sight of this in the *Brown Shoe* case, when it condemned the formation of a larger company by merger because the new firm would be able to offer "lower prices or higher quality for the same price," and this would harm independent shoe sellers.[10] This is an important lesson when we think about big tech, where most firms are big precisely because customers prefer them.

Market Power and Efficiencies

The term "efficiency" refers to things that either reduce a firm's costs or enable it to increase customer satisfaction at the same costs. That could include cost-saving technology, economies of large-scale production, or economies that result from R&D or reorganization, including vertical integration. Few people dispute that these are fundamentally good things. At the same time, however, measuring efficiencies can be extremely difficult, and their importance in antitrust litigation is controversial. The hardest cases are the ones where a practice such as a merger simultaneously increases a firm's market power but also reduces its costs. In the 1960s the economist Oliver E. Williamson proposed that we think of this problem as a welfare "trade-off," or cost-benefit analysis of net effects. In the 1970s antitrust

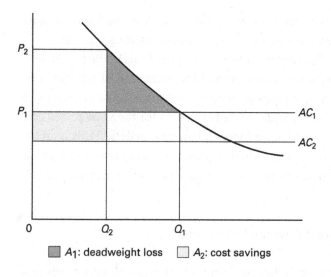

P_2
P_1
AC_1
AC_2
0 Q_2 Q_1

⬛ A_1: deadweight loss ⬜ A_2: cost savings

Figure 2

scholar Robert Bork picked up this idea and illustrated it with the graph shown in figure 2, which he adapted from Williamson.[11]

Bear with me if you are allergic to economic figures. This one illustrates what happens when a practice simultaneously creates market power but also reduces a firm's costs. The analysis would be similar if instead of lower costs the practice led to a better-quality product. The practice could be a merger, a joint venture with a research component, or something else. For simplicity we will think of a merger.

The downward-sloping curve represents demand and shows that as prices (P, the vertical line on the left) come down, output (Q, the horizontal line across the bottom) increases. In this case the merger increases the firm's market power, enabling it to reduce output from Q_1 back to Q_2. In the process, it raises its prices from P_1 to P_2. However, this merger also reduces the firm's costs from horizontal line AC_1 to AC_2. Bork did not explain what these cost savings were.

This merger produces the two shaded areas in the figure. The first, designated A_1, is the "deadweight loss" that accompanies monopoly. A_1 measures the loss to consumers from higher prices as well as reduced output. This loss is a principal reason that we think monopoly is harmful. By contrast, the rectangle A_2 measures the efficiency, or "cost savings," that results from the lower costs. In the model, one can assess the harm or benefit caused by this merger by comparing the two shaded figures. As the deadweight loss triangle becomes larger, the merger is more costly. On the other hand, as the cost savings rectangle becomes larger, the merger is more economically beneficial.

Williamson quite accurately called this a "welfare trade-off" model for determining antitrust liability. It measures the harm to consumers (A_1) against increased efficiency, the gains (A_2) from which were mainly pocketed by the firms. However, Bork added decades of confusion by renaming it a "consumer welfare" model—even though consumers were actually being harmed. As a result of this merger, prices are actually higher and output is actually lower. Bork reasoned that eventually the firm would compete these higher profits away, so ultimately consumers would benefit.

The model exhibits problems that make it undesirable and even unusable. First, making the required measurements is extraordinarily difficult, limiting its application. Second, the figure assumes a market that was competitive prior to a merger but a monopoly after. In most challenged mergers the market was something less than competitive prior to the merger and something less than a monopoly after. For example, a merger of two firms with market shares of 20 percent each would very likely be challenged today, but in that case the post-merger market share is 40 percent, not 100 percent. Because this merger enables collusion or oligopoly by changing the market's structure, the entire market experiences the loss represented by A_1. However, the efficiencies are specific to the merging firms and thus cover only 40 percent of the market's output. In that case the figure understates the net loss caused by this merger by two and a half times!

Another serious problem with the welfare trade-off model has to do with the unexplained source of the efficiencies. Bork's figure uses a horizontal line, falling from AC_1 to AC_2, to illustrate the cost savings, but with no clue about where these savings come from. This is sometimes called the "blackboard economics" fallacy, or the fallacy of thinking that if you can draw a picture of something on a blackboard, it must represent something that exists in the real world. Drawing a line and labeling it "cost savings" is not the same thing as actually producing a lower-cost technology or process. In this case, a result of this merger is that output falls from Q_1 back to Q_2, which is roughly half the distance back to zero. In other words, this firm was able to attain these unexplained efficiencies even as it was cutting its output by half. That number could be either greater than or less than half.

Most of the economies that result from mergers or other practices are economies of scale, which means that costs go down as output goes up. In addition, fixed costs, or per unit costs for things like durable plant and equipment or research, decrease when output goes up. Nearly every large firm experiences fixed costs to some degree. However, these costs *increase* as output goes down. That creates a puzzle: what type of practice or structure enables costs to go down even as output is also going down? They are very likely rare and would have to be proven. Bork's diagram, which describes situations that rarely exist in the real world, is not a very valuable policy tool.

A more realistic rule is that efficiencies should be calculated and included in our evaluation of a practice, but only if the efficiencies are provable (not simply illustrated in a drawing) and are so substantial that the price will be no higher and output no lower than they were prior to the merger. That is in fact the position taken in the Antitrust Division's Merger Guidelines, which the enforcement agencies use to evaluate mergers.[12] A merger will be permitted only if proven efficiencies are sufficient to prevent prices from increasing at all, so there is nothing to trade off. That definition also fits more easily into a properly defined concept of consumer welfare: the merger produces efficiencies, and consumers are unharmed.

Finally, the model assumes that mere wealth transfers are neutral, because losses to one group (consumers) are offset by gains to another group (producers). While this assumption is conventional in traditional economics, it is a contentious issue in most legal policy. One important point is that antitrust is a very poor wealth transfer device. It does not operate like tax or welfare law and specifically target groups for benefits or burdens. Its fundamental goal is to make the pie bigger, not to decide how it should be divided.

Market Power, Patents, and Other Intellectual Property Rights

Large digital firms invest heavily in developing or acquiring intellectual property (IP), including patents, copyrights, and trademarks. Historically the courts often referred to these rights as "monopolies." In fact, the term "patent monopoly" appears in nearly 2,400 U.S. court decisions (as of 2023).

But is a patent really a monopoly? Only rarely. A patent is the right to exclude someone from the technology it covers. It operates much more like a boundary on a parcel of land. Whether the power to exclude someone from entering or using property creates a monopoly depends on the value and uniqueness of the property, not simply on the boundary. For example, a deed giving exclusive rights to a mountain pass that has room for only one railroad line could be extremely valuable and might even create a monopoly in transportation. By contrast, a boundary on a midwestern farm probably does not create any market power at all. Everything the farm can produce is done in competitive markets.

The question of patent market power is also very technology-specific. For example, important drugs are often based on patented molecules, and sometimes a single molecule can create considerable market power. One example is ibuprofen, whose original patent was granted in 1962. Another is glyphosate, a general herbicide patented in 1971 and marketed as Roundup. During the life of their patents, these products had a commanding market presence—glyphosate somewhat more than ibuprofen, which had better alternatives.

At the other extreme are information technology patents, which tend to be very narrow in relation to the final

But is a patent really a monopoly? Only rarely. A patent is the right to exclude someone from the technology it covers. It operates much more like a boundary on a parcel of land.

product. For example, no one knows how many patents are contained in an iPhone, but estimates run from 200 to thousands. Why the ambiguity? Thousands of patents are relevant in some way to iPhone's diverse technologies, including basic calling features, data storage, display functions, internet access and modem, the camera, and so on. However, before we know exactly how many patents an iPhone contains, we need to know how many of those patents it practices—that is, how many valid patents cover specific technological elements in the iPhone. That typically requires a court to determine, first, whether a patent is valid, and second, whether it was infringed. For the vast majority of patents that an iPhone might use, these questions have never been answered. Further, the average patent infringement case, where these questions are addressed, costs more than $2 million. About 95 percent of patent cases settle out of court. Of the ones that go to trial and are fully contested, plaintiffs win less than half, although the number varies widely with the technology.[13]

A few patents, such as the powerful herbicide glyphosate, created significant market power until they expired. Most others do not, and for several reasons. Some are too impractical to use. Others are invalid. Others cover some actual technology, but it is easy to "invent around" them by doing something in a slightly different way. Still others offer a technological alternative that is no better than the public domain technology they seek to displace. Many contribute some minor element of product differentiation to a good but do not significantly improve its competitive standing.

Other types of IP protection are even less likely to create substantial monopoly, although there are some exceptions. Copyrighted code is one possibility. Copyright protection lasts much longer (seventy years plus the life of the author) than patent protection (roughly twenty years). But the same thing is true here as of patents. If the digital program that is copyrighted is not worth much, then neither is the copyright. For example, this author's master's thesis is copyrighted but lies unpublished in a Texas library. Not much market power there. By contrast, the copyrighted code for Microsoft Windows creates a great deal of power. The price of Windows would immediately crash if Windows suddenly lost copyright protection. Digital code can be copied quickly and cheaply, making copyright protection essential, and Windows is a market-dominating product.

Trademarks can serve as entry barriers when customers attach importance to a particular brand or popular name. For example, the patent on glyphosate expired several years ago. Today, anyone can manufacture glyphosate, but only Monsanto/Bayer can call that product "Roundup." How much market power a trademark confers varies—probably very little in most cases, but much more in a few.

When Must Market Power Be Measured? The Per Se Rule

Because of antitrust law's wish to limit monopoly, market power is always relevant in an antitrust case. This distinguishes antitrust law from other areas such as tort, property, or contract law. These are all concerned with individual harms rather than harm to markets as a whole.

This does not mean, however, that market power must be measured in every case. Sometimes it can be inferred from circumstances. Take simple price fixing. Two or more firms simply agree to charge a certain price, without integrating any part of their production or research. Such an agreement grants no benefits to anyone other than the price fixers themselves. Further, it is profitable only if it represents an exercise of market power: the cartel members must have the power to raise prices or their agreement will fail. This is not necessarily true of mergers or the formation of joint ventures. For those, profitability may depend on the participants' ability to reduce costs or produce a better product. To be sure, the cartel members might be mistaken, thinking they have market power when they really do not. But since they are not doing any good either, we don't really need to worry about false condemnation.

Today "naked" price fixing, market division, and boycotts are illegal per se. The term "naked" means that the agreement is not accompanied by any form of integration or joint productive activity. While a fair amount of dispute goes into the question *whether* a restraint is naked, once it is found to be so, no market definition or proof of market power is necessary. A violation can be inferred from the simple conduct alone.

The Rule of Reason

Now let's consider another type of agreement among competitors. Suppose that five computer repair technicians in Los Angeles organize and open an office jointly, calling themselves Computer Associates, Inc. Los Angeles contains thousands of computer fixers, and these five could not conceivably raise market prices. Instead, the members profit by reducing expenses through such things as sharing a building, office management, and insurance, as well as expensive diagnostic equipment. They may even agree on prices for individual services so that they can quote a common rate to prospective customers. None of this sounds like it should be an antitrust violation. The difference is that the profitability of Computer Associates does not depend on the members' ability to fix higher prices but rather on their joint ability to reduce costs or offer better services.

These facts indicate that an antitrust challenge to Computer Associates must be treated under antitrust's "rule of reason," which applies to agreements that incorporate a significant potential for reducing costs or improving quality. Justice Brandeis is often described as the inventor of the rule of reason, which he applied to approve an agreement among members of the Chicago Board of Trade to set the prices of after-hours trading. Justice Brandeis observed that there was no evidence that the rule reduced output, and there seemed to be valid explanations for it.[14]

Today the rule of reason involves four possible stages of analysis, although most decisions never get past the first two. First, the plaintiff must prove market power—usually by showing that the participants collectively control a large market share. In the hypothetical Computer Associates case, that would end it. Its market share of less than 1 percent is too small. As a result, it is implausible that its purpose or likely effect is higher prices or reduced quality.

If the defendants are found to have significant market power, typically a market share of 30 percent or more, then the second query is whether any of the practices raises a significant threat of competitive harm. It would be very hard to make such a showing about the sharing of a building or diagnostic equipment, but Computer Associates' price agreement might require a closer look. In a third stage the computer technicians would have a chance to justify it. Here, the price fix very likely has a harmless explanation. Customers don't hire a particular technician; they simply bring computers in to have them repaired, and the price quote must be one that applies to whoever is assigned that particular repair. Computer Associates cannot easily do that without an agreement about prices.

If the computer technicians succeed in proving a justification, then the challenger still has a chance to show that the benefits could have been obtained by a less restrictive alternative. That seems unlikely in this case.

As these steps suggest, the rule of reason is cumbersome and costly. Most plaintiffs lose rule of reason cases. Very likely, many anticompetitive practices survive antitrust attacks simply because the cases are too difficult to prove. For this reason, reform of the rule of reason remains an important item on the antitrust agenda. Proof needs to be made simpler, but without condemning socially useful practices.

One might ask, why a market power requirement, with its technical computations of relevant markets and market share? The antitrust statutes say nothing about these things. The answer is that they are "forensic" tools used in litigation to measure things that the statute requires. For example, every state has homicide laws that punish people for "causing" the death of another. None of these laws refers to ballistics, fingerprints, or DNA; however, today these are universally used tools for determining who is responsible. That is the best way to think of the technical tools of antitrust enforcement. They help us assess whether a particular harm such as monopoly is likely.[15]

Switching Costs and Barriers to Entry

Market power is a firm's ability to insist on a high price or low quality without losing too many sales. Although customers may complain, something hinders them from switching away. A "switching cost" is the cost someone faces making a change from one product or service to another. Consider these examples:

1. The owner of a computer operating Microsoft Windows and unhappy with Windows' features can switch to a different operating system, but only by getting a different computer, such as an Apple Mac.

2. Both Apple and Android require owners of mobile phones to purchase apps through the phone provider's own stores—the App Store for the iPhone and Google Play for the Android. The owner of an iPhone can avoid this only by changing phones, but Android phones have the same policies.

3. Facebook is free to users, but someone who wants to switch from Facebook to an alternative social networking site will lose her built-up history of friends, messages, contacts, photos, and videos because no common format exists for transferring these from one network to another. This lack of "data portability" operates as a switching cost that increases the longer one has been a Facebook user.

4. Someone using Google Search and unhappy with the results can instantly switch to DuckDuckGo, Bing, or another search engine. Switching on some handheld devices is modestly more difficult than switching on a larger computer.

5. Someone shopping for a new toaster on Amazon and unhappy with Amazon's price or product selection can click away and switch to eBay, Home Depot, or numerous other online sellers. These sellers are smaller than Amazon, but the customer, after all, is looking for just one toaster.

6. Someone unhappy with Walmart's toaster price or selection can drive to a different store.

7. Someone who is unhappy with Microsoft Word's purchase price can switch to Google Docs; this will require learning some new commands and different capabilities, and the conversion of existing documents is sometimes imperfect.

These are examples of switching costs. Many raise issues similar to our earlier discussion of lock-in in the *Kodak* case. That is, switching costs may be high because a user has made a previous commitment to a particular product. For example, for someone who already owns a computer running Microsoft Windows, switching to the

Mac OS is more costly than for someone making an entry level choice of which computer to buy.

Sometimes switching costs make switching take a longer time. Sometimes they effectively prevent switching because the gains to be achieved are less than the cost of switching. In some cases, such as Google Search, switching costs are extremely low. A dissatisfied user can switch immediately, without losing paid-up commitments or paying the costs of buying a new device or signing up for a new service. You can walk up to a totally strange computer in a library and conduct a Google search without inputting any personal or financial information. Alphabet's very large market share (90+ percent) in Google Search is very likely not a result of high user switching costs.

As the examples indicate, computer operating systems can be a bottleneck. They often commit users to particular devices. Arrangements that bundle other services to the operating system can be similar. The *Epic Games* case is a recent example.[16] An iPhone user can purchase Epic Games and extra levels only through the App Store, where Apple charges a large commission. Here, a rule change creating more competition on the platform could benefit consumers, although the court of appeals did not see it that way. In the previously discussed *Kodak* decision the lock-in resulted from design incompatibilities. The Kodak machine used only Kodak-specific parts. By contrast, in *Epic Games* the lock-in results from a policy that

Apple could change by providing alternatives to Appstore purchases.

Examples 5 and 6, concerning the unhappy Amazon and Walmart customers, illustrate one of the irrationalities of proposed federal legislation that would limit "self preferencing," but only on internet sales. The term refers to how large online platforms display or otherwise preference the goods of third parties. In fact, customer switching costs are usually higher in the traditional brick-and-mortar world than on the internet. To be sure, they may not be all that high on either one. Things like shopping malls enable customers to have access to many stores in a short walk. Nevertheless, switching costs are typically even lower on the internet, and even large firms like Amazon have numerous rivals. That is not true of every product, but it is true of most. For example, a customer seeking a new toaster and unhappy with Amazon's offerings can readily click to target.com, kohls.com, homedepot.com, or kitchen aid.com without leaving her computer.

Some switching costs can impose significant limits on consumers. In others cases they are low, making monopoly prices difficult to sustain. Even when switching costs are high, not every limit on them is anticompetitive. For example, Apple has consistently argued that the need to maintain security requires it to control its App Store by excluding third-party transactions. Such claims need to be proven. One important historical case is AT&T. Prior to the breakup of the phone monopoly, AT&T argued strenuously that any "foreign attachment" hooked into the phone system would jeopardize its operation. That claim turned out to be wildly exaggerated. Today hundreds of firms make devices or provide services that connect to the phone system.

Closely related to switching costs are "barriers to entry," which concerns suppliers rather than customers. Classical economics made a strong assumption that any firm's attempt to charge monopoly prices would attract new competitors. As new firms came in and added their output, the price would come down. As a result, in the long run markets would always move toward competition. However, as the British economist John Maynard Keynes famously said, "In the long run we are all dead." Legal policy cannot just walk away from an issue, confident that in the long run the situation will correct itself. Depending on how long that run is, the cost of monopoly can be quite high.

If entry really is easy and quick, then monopoly prices are unlikely to be durable. Suppose someone starts washing cars in his driveway and, seeing no competitors, charges $100 for a fifteen-minute wash. Hearing this, many people decide to start washing cars for profit themselves. They don't need a license, and the only equipment is a hose, a bucket, a cloth, and a brush. Soon the market will be flooded with competitors and the price will fall quickly.

If entry really is easy and quick, then monopoly prices are unlikely to be durable.

If entry barriers are extremely low, as they probably are for manual car washing in one's driveway, then even a person with a large market share would not be able to charge monopoly prices for long. In most markets entry takes longer and is more costly. Construction of a plant and design of a product such as an automobile or microprocessor can take years. Further, the failure rate of new businesses is high, so the risk of a loss must be calculated in. For example, 80 percent of new Manhattan restaurants close within five years, and for some of those entry can cost millions of dollars. If a market already has many sellers, then we need not worry much about entry barriers. But if there are only a few, then competitive prices may depend on the possibility of ongoing entry to keep them low.

Courts have found the following things to be high barriers to entry: portfolios of patents and other IP rights, licensing requirements and costs, scarcity of suitable sites, or the need for highly specialized equipment and facilities. For networked markets such as Facebook, a built-up user base can also be a formidable barrier, as can network effects that give larger networks advantages over smaller ones.

Human Behavior and Market Power

Neoclassical economics, which remains the dominant approach to antitrust economics, assumes that economic decision-makers have a defined set of preferences and act rationally to maximize them. By contrast, *behavioral economics* tries to incorporate biological accounts of human nature that are both more complex and less consistent. When they are allowed, they can be quite relevant to antitrust policy.

For example, people answering opinion polls often state positions opposing big retailers and favoring family businesses. By contrast, their buying behavior is much more favorable toward larger firms. Further, customers do not always choose the lowest price, or make what appears to be the objectively best choice. Shopping behavior is actually very diverse, both physically and online. Shoppers can be searchers, impulse buyers, brand-loyal buyers, bargain hunters, in-and-out, and even perpetual browsers. They can also be well educated about a product or completely uninformed, simply observing what others are doing. Whether some of this conduct is "irrational" or simply reflects a different set of priorities is hard to say and, thankfully, beyond the scope of this book.[17]

Making rules for every unexplained variation in consumer behavior would result in antitrust's wheels grinding to a halt. Antitrust market share numbers provide one way of slicing through this by simply asking what is the range of *realistic alternatives* that a market provides. That is, antitrust law examines power and exclusion by looking at the objective availability of choices. It generally does not try to account for individual differences in consumer taste or behavior. If we observe that 23 percent of coffee makers are sold by Amazon, or that Amazon's own customers select Amazon's house brand 15 percent of the time, those numbers tell us very little about the variety of strategies and impulses that guide customer choice. They do, however, tell us what the *aggregated* results of these strategies are. Some customers may strongly prefer house brands; others avoid them at all costs or prefer a particular brand. Others go into each transaction with no inclination in either direction. The relevant question for antitrust is not what motivates their shopping strategies but what their realistic options are.

Are there times when a specific idiosyncrasy of consumer behavior should warrant antitrust attention? Perhaps. Maybe customers as a group are not efficient searchers. Perhaps they make too many impulsive decisions. Should antitrust make special rules for these? We should understand that (1) protecting the behavior reduces the incentive to change it, and (2) identifying a class of behavior for special treatment will invite many disputes about measurement and scope. For example, when Amazon ranks product offerings in its "buy box," it makes a choice. Ascending price is best only if the products and terms are identical in all other respects. Any amount of differentiation among sellers makes the ranking at least somewhat subjective. In fact, most Amazon customers purchase Amazon's own designated first choice. Does that mean that Amazon is manipulating customers, or simply predicting what their behavior will be? Or, alternatively, does it simply indicate that customers as a group have high confidence in Amazon's rankings and see no reason to deviate? For the most part, antitrust ignores these issues and focuses on the options that the market realistically makes available. If customers are free to choose without significant limitation, we can be less fussy about the menu that is presented to them.

Two-Sided Platforms, Attention Markets, and Winner-Take-All

Assessing the market power of large digital platforms such as Amazon, Alphabet, Apple, or Meta is challenging for several reasons. First, they offer "clusters" of products that do not compete with one another. Cluster markets were discussed earlier in this chapter. Further, the market share of the platform may be quite different from the market share of the individual products. For example, Amazon is a very large retailer, and it controls a significant share of the market for eBooks. It is also a very large streamer of movie and television content, but it has several rivals of roughly the same size. For more tactile products most of its market shares are much smaller—for example, about 20 percent of small kitchen appliances and less than 3 percent of groceries. Someone searching for a toaster has considerably more choices of a seller than someone searching for ebooks.

These numbers are important because for most purposes, market power attaches to particular products, not to the firm as a whole. For example, Microsoft is a very large firm with large market shares in its Windows operating system and Office suite. However, it has less than 1 percent of the market for smartphone operating systems and (at this writing) 3 percent in its Bing search engine. Its market power in the Windows OS makes monopolization plausible, but not its OS market share in smartphones or its share of search engines. Or suppose the claim is that Amazon is engaging in "self-preferencing" or some other practice intended to switch customers to Amazon's own Amazon Basics electric toaster rather than competing sellers. The plausibility of this scheme and of anticompetitive results depends more on Amazon's presence in the toaster market, not so much on Amazon's overall size. Amazon's power over toasters depends on how readily customers can click away to a different toaster on Amazon or can leave Amazon altogether for a different seller.

The ebook problem is messier, partly because ebooks need digital readers. Suppose Amazon is steering customers to its own ebooks rather than to those supplied by other vendors. Here, Amazon's share of the ebook market is roughly 68 percent (as of mid-2022). ebooks compete

For most purposes market power attaches to particular products, not to the firm as a whole.

with conventional books, and ebooks make up a little over 25 percent of the entire book market. Amazon also sells the Kindle book format. Although files can be converted to other formats, such as ePub, books by default are sold on Amazon in four different formats: hardback, paperback, audiobook, and Kindle. Someone who wishes to purchase an ebook on Amazon is strongly steered to Amazon's own Kindle format. Of course, one can also readily switch to an alternative seller of ebooks, such as eBooks.com, barne sandnoble.com, or kobo.com. Further, Amazon licenses a Kindle app at no charge so that people can read Kindle books on non-Amazon devices, such as an iPad or even desktops and laptops with Windows. Overall, the ebook market would likely benefit from more interoperability or a larger number of distributors of the same format. Nevertheless, it is hardly clear that ebook purchasers are unreasonably constrained.

Another issue, one that antitrust law is just starting to work out, concerns "two-sided" markets, discussed in the introduction. Many two-sided platforms, such as Facebook or Google Search, are free on one side but supported mainly by advertising on the other. Even nominally free services have a price, however, which is the user's *attention*. That is what advertisers are willing to pay for.[18] In a world where people are bombarded with information, being able to get people's attention is valuable. Further, the attention market is highly competitive. The owners of successful "free" platforms such as Facebook and X (for-merly Twitter) put substantial resources into making the user experience attractive, even addictive. At this writing antitrust law has not significantly incorporated these insights. Further, it is not clear that doing so would require significant legal changes. To be sure, cartels or mergers that make customer attention more costly or less valuable should receive antitrust scrutiny, but the law already does this by focusing on quality in addition to price. For example, Facebook's acquisition of Instagram did not raise user's nominal prices, but it did blunt competition between the two for user attention.

Occasionally people claim that the large digital platforms are "winner-take-all," or natural monopoly markets. That is certainly not the case for most of them, although it may be true for a few. Today, the United States has more than 7,000 magazines and roughly 1,250 daily newspapers. Most of these have a digital version, and some are available exclusively in digital format. Overall, few two-sided platforms are winner-take-all. The main reason is product differentiation, which is very substantial in digital markets. Could a new firm enter Facebook's market with a perfect clone? Very likely not. Facebook has too big a head start, and few people would switch to an upstart that promised nothing that Facebook did not already have.

But, as figure 3 suggests, that is not where Facebook faces new entry. The new entrants will not be clones but

Figure 3

rather new firms with distinctive products. For example, both X (as Twitter, 2006) and TikTok (2016) are younger than Facebook (2004). LinkedIn (2002) is a little older. These firms succeed because they offer features and appearance distinguishable from Facebook's. They appeal to a somewhat different audience. This threat of entry from differentiated rivals very likely accounts for many of the hundreds of acquisitions that the platforms have made of new digital firms, including Facebook's 2012 acquisition of Instagram. At the time Instagram had thirteen employees. To be blunt, Facebook was trying to get rid of a rival that threatened to mature into a significant competitor. This problem will be considered in the next chapter.

Another thing that complicates the measurement of market power on two-sided markets is that demand and revenue often come from different sides, making the measurement of markups more difficult. For example, Google Search is free to users but costly to advertisers. One cannot measure markups without looking at both sides. A few two-sided platforms, such as credit cards, even have a negative price on one side. You might own a Visa card that gives you 2 percent cash back on your purchases. In fact, that rebate is financed by the merchant, whose payment for accepting the Visa card includes the payment to the card holder. Overall margins can be calculated only by looking at both sides.[19]

The next chapter considers the types of conduct that can create market power, enable its exercise, or prolong its duration.

ANTICOMPETITIVE CONDUCT
AND BIG TECH

Simply being a monopolist is not an antitrust violation. Nor is bigness itself unlawful. Rather, a violation requires proof of both market power and anticompetitive conduct. The exception is for per se unlawful conduct such as price fixing, where market power is assumed. Once bad conduct is shown, the arsenal of antitrust remedies is very broad, as the next chapter describes.

Many people are concerned that big tech firms have too much power. "Power" can mean different things. Market power, the subject of chapter 2, is the power to charge monopoly prices. By contrast, political power could be the power to influence government institutions or voters in inappropriate ways. We may also speak of the "power" to deceive or to discriminate based on ideology or belief, to influence opinion, or to disseminate pornography or other indecent matter. But antitrust does not rule the entire world of bad conduct. We have plenty of laws for doing these things. In any event, nothing in the text of the antitrust laws justifies going beyond concerns about competition and monopoly.

Antitrust's legitimate concerns include the power to raise prices by reducing market output, to restrain innovation, or to exclude rivals or other firms that threaten to become substantial rivals. Congress can always broaden the scope of antitrust law if it wishes, but for most problems it would do better to use other legal rules, such as communications law, lobbying law, environmental law, or tort law. Even when the Clayton Antitrust Act was passed during the height of the Progressive Era, Congress doubled down on economic concerns, including only practices that "may substantially lessen competition" or that "tend to create a monopoly."

Legally, antitrust law treats claims against big tech firms just as it treats the anticompetitive conduct of other firms. Big tech firms do have a few unique features, however. First, as noted previously, many of them operate in two-sided markets. For example, Google Search and Facebook are both free to users. They get their revenue from the other side of the platform, which is principally advertisers. This can complicate the analysis of certain practices, such as anticompetitive pricing, and also the measurement of market power.

Antitrust's legitimate concerns include the power to raise prices by reducing market output, to restrain innovation, or to exclude rivals or other firms that threaten to become substantial rivals.

Another common feature of many big tech platforms is digital content, which has a much different cost and production structure than traditional content does. This issue has come up in the context of ebooks. Later we consider claims that Amazon has priced ebooks too low.

Yet another feature that is not entirely unique to big tech is networking. Tech markets often require more coordination among participants than do more traditional markets. Networks typically become more valuable as the number of users increases. This is particularly important when we consider the effects of breaking up networked firms. For example, if we "break up" Facebook by (1) dividing it into discrete geographic zones, or (2) segregating users (such as men on one platform and women on another), or (3) forcing it to spin off specific features, such as video posting, the main thing we accomplish is harm to the user experience. We have certainly made Facebook "smaller," but not in any socially valuable way. Breaking things is easy. Restructuring them in a way that furthers the antitrust interest in competitive markets, not so much.

This chapter is divided into four parts. First is the meaning of "harm to competition," which antitrust law requires. The second is monopolization, with its focus on unilateral conduct by market dominating firms, including digital firms. Next are anticompetitive agreements. Finally are mergers.

The Nature of Competitive Injury

In the 1970s Pueblo Bowl-O-Mat was an independently owned bowling alley in Pueblo, Colorado. It was doing reasonably well at a time when interest in bowling was in decline. Belmont Lanes, its principal competitor, was struggling to pay its bills and in danger of shutting down. Belmont's biggest creditor was Brunswick, the nation's largest supplier of bowling equipment. Brunswick inaugurated a program of purchasing lanes that were falling behind on their loan payments. Brunswick acquired Belmont Lanes and made a major investment in improving its building and equipment. As a result, Bowl-O-Mat now faced a rejuvenated competitor, largely killing its chances of becoming the dominant lanes in Pueblo. It sued Brunswick under the antitrust laws, claiming that the acquisition of Belmont Lanes was an unlawful merger.

Bowl-O-Mat's antitrust complaint made antitrusters scratch their heads. It claimed that it would have experienced significant growth and perhaps even become a monopoly in Pueblo, except for Brunswick's revival of its competitor. That was too much even for Justice Thurgood Marshall, a liberal who strongly favored aggressive antitrust enforcement. The purpose of the antitrust laws, he wrote, is not to preserve monopolistic structures for the protection of one competitor. Rather, they seek to promote competition. Bowl-O-Mat was actually complaining about more rather than less competition.[1]

The *Brunswick* rule says that a plaintiff must show more than simple harm to itself from an antitrust violation. It must also show "antitrust injury," which is injury consistent with the antitrust goal of promoting competition. Practices that increase output, yield lower prices, or either facilitate or reflect greater investment or innovation should not be antitrust violations simply because they injure one or more competitors.

The antitrust injury story tells a cautionary tale when we think about antitrust violations in big tech. Overall, big tech companies are highly innovative firms. Their prices are usually low, and they enjoy high customer satisfaction. They have made outsize contributions to economic growth, and overall they are good places to work. Many of them entered the market on the strength of some new product or innovation that customers love. But they do often injure competitors or smaller firms. For example, the rise of digital commerce has devastated Main Street. Further, even within digital commerce large firms often have big advantages over small ones. To be sure, they have engaged in several anticompetitive practices as well. But intelligent antitrust policy must take some pains to distinguish practices that really harm *competition* from those that merely hurt a *competitor*. If some individual firms are hurt but the market overall is actually producing more, with better

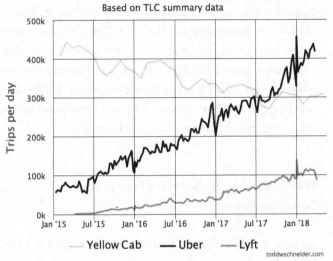

NYC Daily Trips: Yellow Cab, Uber, and Lyft
Based on TLC summary data

Trips per day

500k
400k
300k
200k
100k
0k

Jan '15   Jul '15   Jan '16   Jul '16   Jan '17   Jul '17   Jan '18

······ Yellow Cab   —— Uber   —— Lyft

toddwschneider.com

Figure 4

products and lower prices, that provides a poor basis for an antitrust violation.

Consider what happened in New York when Uber and Lyft began competing with traditional Yellow Cabs. Figure 4 shows that when the ride-sharing apps entered New York City in 2015 the market share of traditional taxis declined, while that of Uber and Lyft increased. However, the competitiveness of the overall market is the *sum* of the three providers (assuming no one else is in the market). That sum, taken by adding the vertical distances of the three lines at the extreme right side, is quite a bit higher than taxi sales were at the time of entry. While the traditional taxis were clearly injured, the overall taxi market experienced higher output, providing more rides to customers and more opportunities for drivers. Uber's entry does not make a good case for an antitrust violation. While there was harm to traditional taxis, both customers and drivers benefited from higher volume and lower prices.

Monopolization: Exclusionary Practices by Dominant Firms

Section 2 of the Sherman Antitrust Act makes it unlawful to "monopolize" or attempt to monopolize. The antitrust laws never define these terms. When the statute was passed in 1890 the term "monopoly" referred to exclusive rights created by governments, including patents, and a fair amount of litigation had addressed the legality of these grants. But section 2 targeted practices that did not involve a government grant, including below cost pricing, anticompetitive acquisitions of competitors, exclusive agreements, and anticompetitive uses of technology or intellectual property (IP). The courts began a process, now more than a century-long, of identifying the various forms of bad conduct that might be unlawful monopolization.

In addition to bad conduct, the monopolization offense also requires that a firm have a dominant position in its market. Today, that requirement hovers at around a minimum 60 percent share of a relevant market. That number has not changed much since the 1940s. Someone suing a firm for monopolization must establish both the "power" requirement and the "conduct" requirement. Both have led to significant litigation, making monopolization cases very costly. The government enforcement agencies, which always operate under budget limitations, must therefore choose wisely.

Monopolization can be both offensive and defensive. The offensive version is the one we usually think of, which is using harmful practices in order to create a monopoly. The defensive one, often called "monopoly maintenance," is the use of anticompetitive practices to protect a dominant position that the monopolist already has. For example, insofar as Facebook already had a dominant position, one way to look at its purchases of Instagram and WhatsApp is as attempts to protect Facebook's position from increased competition. The *Microsoft* case twenty years earlier was much the same. Microsoft already had a dominant position with the Windows operating system but feared that the Netscape web browser would become an avenue for developing competing operating systems or programs that could take over operating system functions.

Both types of monopolization are unlawful and the standards for challenging them are similar.

The discussion that follows examines the main conduct claims that have been brought against dominant firms under section 2, focusing on big tech. Keep in mind, however, that antitrust law does not have distinctive rules for big tech. The rules are the same, but application differs with the facts.

Refusal to Deal and Self-Preferencing

While antitrust law prohibits many boycotts, or agreements not to deal with a third party, unilateral refusals to deal are treated very differently. Within the Anglo-American economic tradition, each firm is presumed to stand on its own feet and may not insist on aid from its competitors. For example, if a computer manufacturer has difficulty locating processor chips, it can certainly agree that another firm will supply them. However, that firm has no antitrust obligation to sell chips if it does not want to.

The Supreme Court's 1985 *Aspen Skiing* decision recognized a narrow exception to this rule. Highlands, the smaller of two downhill skiing companies in Aspen, Colorado, had previously joined a marketing venture with the dominant firm, Aspen Skiing. While the two firms each maintained their own facilities, the venture sold a popular "all-Aspen" lift ticket that combined access to both firms' slopes and ski lifts. Then, without a good explanation, the larger firm abandoned the venture. The termination injured the smaller Highlands much more than Aspen Skiing, and Highlands sued under the antitrust laws. The Supreme Court held that an unjustified *withdrawal* from a joint arrangement could establish an antitrust violation. The *Aspen* rule is narrow, however. It does not create any duty to share assets, but only a duty not to terminate an existing voluntary sharing arrangement anticompetitively. Two decades later the court held that if there was no voluntary sharing agreement from the beginning, a plaintiff did not have a right to seek one.[2]

Today this law seems excessively restrictive for information technologies. Networks such as the wired and wireless phone system, the internet, and autonomous vehicles depend critically on sharing of resources. The empirical literature indicates that dominant firms in such networks frequently have incentives to limit interconnection with smaller firms if they can keep that business to themselves. Nevertheless, the existing antitrust law is pretty clear: firms have no general duty to interconnect with rivals.

The other side of the coin is that an overly aggressive sharing rule may provide an excuse for some firms to free ride on investments made by other firms. For that reason, the courts have been reluctant to extend dealing duties too far. For example, Walmart might purchase and resell Teakhaus kitchen cutting boards if it wishes. If it refuses, however, Teakhaus has no antitrust claim against Walmart. Further, Walmart is entitled to select among its suppliers. The Census of Manufactures identifies 184 makers of kitchen cutting boards in the United States, and Walmart might also sell them under its Home Trends label. Should it have a duty to sell the boards of all 184 manufacturers? Must it follow any particular rules in determining which ones to carry, or whether to display or promote its own brand over those of other suppliers? May it drop a particular board and substitute another one? May it run a promotion of one particular brand of kitchen products but not others?

Under the antitrust laws, Walmart has a right to do any of these things, provided it is acting unilaterally and the refusal is not unlawful for some other reason. For example, in selecting suppliers it may not engage in race or gender discrimination. But it could certainly prefer lower-cost suppliers over higher-cost ones, or products that get better customer reviews or that sell faster. Occupancy of shelf space is a "rental" cost, and retailers universally prefer to stock products that turn over quickly. These rules also apply to Walmart's decision about how to promote and display the cutting boards it has selected for distribution. If it wants to put one in a prominent place at the front of the store, that is entirely its business. This is true over most of commerce. Ford has no duty to sell new cars made by Chrysler. Apple has no duty to sell non-Apple products in its Apple Stores. Häagen-Dazs ice cream stores have no duty to sell Blue Bonnet or Ben & Jerry's. The local grocer is free to select either Chiquita or Del Monte bananas if it does not want to stock both. Of course, nothing prevents them from doing so if they wish to and can get the other firm to agree.

Should the rule be different for an e-retailer such as Amazon, which is roughly the same size as Walmart? Customer ability to switch cannot be the answer. Customers shopping on the internet can usually switch more easily and cheaply than those shopping in traditional stores. Even if one is limited to the internet there is an ample supply of cutting board retailers, including Target, Home Depot, Ikea, the Container Store, and many others. One can only guess, but for nearly any product the number of alternatives within "clicking distance" on the internet is very likely larger than the number within walking or driving distance of a traditional retailer. There is no obvious reason for treating self-preferencing by Amazon more harshly than self-preferencing by Walmart.

The existing law of monopolization already reaches some self-preferencing, as Microsoft's confrontations with Netscape illustrate. In 1995 Microsoft CEO Bill Gates wrote an ominous email to employees, warning them of an "Internet Tidal Wave." For all of Microsoft's embrace of personal computer technology, Windows at the time was built on a fairly old model in which the operating system, programs, and data all resided in the computer's self-contained storage. Telecommunications were largely added on. Many Windows users had landline dial-up for occasional internet checks of email, the stock markets, or other types of external information. The expansion of broadband and the highly innovative Netscape internet browser posed a formidable threat to that system. Gates feared that Netscape would "commoditize the operating system" by pulling some functionality out of the operating system entirely, ultimately enabling computers with different operating systems to communicate with one another. That could blunt Windows' competitive edge.

Nearly everything that Gates foretold in that email eventually came true. With higher-speed communications, increasing functionality, and data moved away from the desktop box and into the cloud, the operating system became less dominant. The ultimate winner was not Netscape but rather Google, which did not even exist when Gates composed his memo.

Microsoft responded to the Netscape threat with a number of practices that were intended not to kill the internet but rather to steer internet traffic toward Microsoft's own browser, Internet Explorer (IE). It bundled IE into the Windows operating system, even consolidating the code into one large program. It also imposed many contractual restrictions on software developers and internet access providers that required them to prefer IE over any alternative browser.

While all this conduct was a form of self-preferencing, most of it was carried out through anticompetitive agreements. One kind was "exclusive dealing," or contracts requiring third parties to deal only with Microsoft's own products. Another was "tying," or Microsoft's insistence that two of its own products (e.g., the operating system and the browser) be used together. That type of self-preferencing, whose effect was to maintain Windows' operating system dominance, is much more extreme than simply choosing to sell one firm's products rather than another. For example, Amazon's suppliers generally do not agree to deal exclusively with Amazon.

So called self-preferencing can come in many varieties. For example:

a. All users of the platform must use a particular secondary product, enforced by license agreements or decisions not to license, such as Apple's insistence that app purchases be made through its own App Store.

b. All users of the platform must use a particular secondary product because computer code makes only this particular product compatible with the platform, as in Apple iPhone's design, which make it very difficult to use a non-Apple operating system.

c. All users of the platform will get a discount if they use the platform's own secondary product rather than some else's.

d. All users of the platform will get a warning that purchase of a secondary product from someone else will void their warranty.

e. When platform users want to purchase a secondary product, the search result favors the platform's own product; for example, an Amazon search for "AAA batteries" may display the Amazon Basics brand first, followed by Duracell, Energizer, and ACDelco. Alternatively, by default, purchasers of a new Windows computer see Microsoft Edge as the default browser. Or perhaps Netflix displays its own self-produced films above films that it licenses from others. However, customers are free to choose among the alternatives at no cost.

f. An internet seller offers both its own products and those of competitors, ranking them by ascending price, descending customer review score, or some other facially neutral system.

Of these practices, (a) through (d) can sometimes be unlawful under antitrust law. Practices (e) and (f) are not. No antitrust rule forbids a firm from offering both its own products and those of others on the same site, and antitrust policy generally encourages it because it creates more competition. That is largely true for both brick-and-mortar retailers and e-retailers. Even the first four practices are not illegal per se, however. Rather, a challenger must show market power and anticompetitive results. Self-preferencing is generally illegal only if it denies customers effective access to substitutes.

Anticompetitive Practices Involving Intellectual Property

High-tech firms both develop and use large amounts of IP—mainly patents, copyrights, and trademarks. The tech industry overall is research-intensive and produces many patents, particularly in internet and telecommunications technologies. All of the largest owners of patents are high-tech firms. The large digital platforms that deal directly with consumers, such as Amazon and Meta (Facebook), are not among the top, however. IBM is the largest patent owner. Samsung, LG, and Canon are numbers 2, 3, and 4. Apple is number 11, largely because of its cellular phone business. Microsoft is number 12, Amazon is number 15, and Alphabet (Google) is number 17. Meta is number 31.[3]

One problem with the patent system is the one-sided nature of patent issuance. The parties to this process are the patent applicant and a government examiner, but not the balance of society, which faces exclusion by an invalid or excessively broad patent. For example, think of a will

No antitrust rule forbids a firm from offering both its own products and those of others on the same site, and antitrust policy generally encourages it because it creates more competition.

contest in which someone argues that stepchildren should be prevented from inheriting, but that excludes the stepchildren from the decision process. The system for granting patents lacks one feature that seems essential to democratic processes, which is that they be "adversarial" when conflicting rights are at stake, permitting input from opponents as well as supporters. In recent years the creation of expanded challenge rights has reduced this problem but not eliminated it.

One result is over-issuance. Tech patents in particular are too numerous. They are also harder to interpret than other patents, leading to more litigation. Relatedly, networking is a bigger presence in digital technologies. As a result, tech firms license to one another much more than do firms in more traditional industries. Cross-licensing and standard-setting requirements in networked industries are prominent and provoke a large amount of litigation.

Product producers can also abuse IP, just as much as IP owners. One claim against Amazon is that it uses information provided by its third-party sellers to copy their products, typically offering them at a lower price. One account widely circulated in the press was that Amazon "reverse engineered" a laptop stand it had been selling for a company named Rain Design, and then sold its own version at a lower price.[4]

The issue here is the obverse of IP protection, which is protection of the public domain. Reverse engineering, or copying, is not illegal if the product is not protected by an IP right. In fact, the point of the Constitution's grant of patents and copyrights for "limited times" was to provide protection from copying for covered goods, but also to ensure the right to copy goods that are not covered. Consistent with this, the Supreme Court has struck down state laws that attempt to protect things that patent law does not protect.[5] In sum, the IP laws are designed to navigate the boundary between two important rights. On one side is encouragement of invention through exclusive rights. On the other is encouragement of wide dissemination through free copying of things that are in the public domain. Overall, a healthy public domain is at least as important as a healthy IP system.

But actual policies can be in conflict. In some areas we are extremely enthusiastic about protection of the public domain. For example, when the patent on a high-value pharmaceutical drug expires, manufacturers, health networks, insurers, and patients all push fiercely to get a generic onto the market as quickly as possible. Encouraging generics is government policy, and we have used the antitrust laws against attempts to delay generic entry.[6]

If Amazon's copying infringes someone else's patent or other IP right, then the answer is an infringement lawsuit. Extending exclusion rights to unprotected products would narrow the public domain. Further, would this policy apply only to Amazon, or also to other firms that copy public domain products?

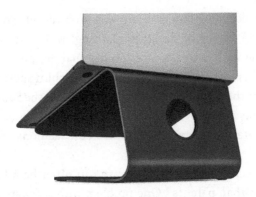

Figure 5

A claim with more bite is that Amazon takes advantage of *confidential* information provided by third-party sellers and uses this to create cheaper versions. That could be a violation of a trade secret or perhaps a contract violation if it is proven. In fact, however, most of the information that someone needs to reverse engineer a product sold on Amazon is already available. Most important is a copy of the product itself, which anyone can purchase. That is all an engineer would need to copy the very simple Rain Design laptop stand (see figure 5).

In addition are posted customer evaluations, also accessible to everyone. To be sure, there could still be other nonpublic information that Amazon might use to make copies, but this would have to be shown. Incidentally, generic house brands of popular products have been around for decades, long before there was an internet. So have knock-off copies of designer clothing, which are often available within weeks after an original design is introduced. In most cases the copyists have nothing more than a copy of the design that they copied. Indeed, the Supreme Court has applied the antitrust laws against an attempt by private designers to keep knock-off fashions off the market.[7]

In tech, copyrighted software can often be a bigger problem than patents.[8] One problem with software copyrights, particularly on computer code, is that they can behave like patents. They protect functions rather than "expression," which is a traditional dividing line between patent and copyright. Nevertheless, copyrighted code obtains the duration that is given to copyrights—typically seventy years plus the life of the author. For this reason, the Supreme Court was wise to hold in *Google v. Oracle* (2021) that copying the functional features of computer code is "fair use," which means that it can be done without a license.[9] That holding limits, but does not eliminate, the extent to which computer code can be a vehicle of market exclusion.

Nearly all the computer code that has ever been placed on the market remains under copyright unless the owners have dedicated it to the public by an open source commitment, or else it was never copyrightable to begin with. Even that oversimplifies the story. For example, Android software drives most of the world's smartphones (roughly 70 percent for Android to roughly 26 percent for Apple's proprietary IOS). Android itself is open source and can be copied freely, but if an Android phone manufacturer wants to install Google Play, which is Google's app store and regarded by most device manufacturers as essential, it must also install Google Search and make it the default search engine. A combination of even open source software and contracts can be unreasonably exclusionary. As of this writing, this practice is coming under antitrust scrutiny.

Anticompetitive Distribution, Including Pricing

To what extent has product distribution by digital platforms harmed traditional retailing? The answer depends on the product and the technology. Purely digital technologies have harmed Main Street severely. That is particularly true of ebooks and the digital streaming of music and video content, which usually bypasses retail stores altogether. Of course, people can still purchase printed books, music CDs, and movie DVDs from retail stores as well as from e-sellers. Nevertheless, retailers such as Walmart and Target, which traditionally sold many DVDs and CDs, have taken an enormous hit. Many smaller retailers that once specialized in CDs and DVDs have been forced to shut down. In 2022 about three times as many songs were streamed as were purchased on hard media such as CDs.[10] DVDs today account for less than 10 percent of the video market. Movie theaters have been harmed as well.[11] The hit on traditional bookstores has not been quite as bad because many more people continue to read physical books; but they have suffered as well.

Brick-and-mortar stores still have advantages in other market categories. These include services such as restaurant dining, hairdressing, lawn care, and therapeutic services. While you can get an appointment for a massage on the internet, the actual massage has to be in person. The market for perishable items such as groceries has experienced more modest injury. For example, Amazon's grocery sales, including those made online through Whole Foods, account for roughly 2.5 percent of U.S. grocery sales. Overall, online grocery sales are about 10 percent of the total. In between these extremes are a host of tactile products where the market shares vary, such as Amazon's market shares of roughly 23 percent for small electrical appliances and 12 percent for clothing. For clothing, traditional stores still have some advantages that online retailers have had difficulty duplicating, such as the ability to try on clothes before purchasing.

We can infer that all of this has been good for consumers from the simple fact that consumers have had the choice and these market shares reflect the consequences. They stream music and videos not because CDs and DVDs are no longer available but because that is their choice, particularly among younger buyers. As a result, it is almost

Purely digital technologies have harmed Main Street severely. That is particularly true of ebooks and the digital streaming of music and video content, which usually bypasses retail stores altogether.

impossible to infer harmful conduct from digital sellers' market shares alone. These differences strongly suggest that the nature of the product and the convenience and preferences of consumers explain much more about the reason why large internet platforms have injured traditional markets. They may not explain everything.

Do large digital platforms engage in predatory or anticompetitive distribution practices? Yes, but they are mainly unreasonably exclusionary contracts, which are addressed later in this chapter.

From its beginning, antitrust law has recognized an offense of "predatory pricing," which is pricing a product so low that it drives competitors out of business. After that the predator raises its price to monopoly levels. Antitrust analysis of predatory pricing has become mired in restrictive technical rules. Most people agree that a predatory price must be "below cost." We do not want to condemn firms simply for having lower costs and then setting a profitable price that competitors are unable to match. The thing about a below-cost price is that it is not sustainable. Eventually the predator must raise the price to a high level in order to recoup the money it lost during predation.

The requirement of prices below cost does raise some issues that are relevant to tech platforms. One is the nature of pricing on two-sided markets. Google Search is free to users, even though it is certainly not costless to supply. But Alphabet, Google Search's owner, is not engaged in predatory pricing. Search is a two-sided market that interacts with users on one side and collects advertising or placement revenue from different entities on the other side. Market two-sidedness is common on digital platform markets, both large and small. Even a relatively small magazine might obtain revenue from two different sources, subscribers and advertisers.

Market two-sidedness is not unique to digital platforms. In fact, markets like this have been around for decades. For example, both over-the-air radio and TV, comparatively old technologies, operate under a model that is free to listeners and viewers but paid for by advertisers on the other side. In 1922 radio station WEAF (later WNBC) in New York aired the first paid radio commercial, which was an advertisement for a local apartment building. The growth of advertiser-supported media has never relented since. A similar model applies to newspapers, magazines, and social networking sites. To determine whether a price on a two-sided market is below cost, someone must look at all of the revenue coming in from all sources. If you do that, you see that Google Search and Facebook are in fact profitable, notwithstanding that their price to most users is zero.

A second pricing issue pertains to digitization, which is a common attribute of tech platforms. Consider books as an example. Some of the costs of traditional book publishing are fixed, which means that the publisher pays them a single time and they do not vary with the number of copies that are sold. These would include author acquisition, manuscript editing and preparation, and the durable equipment such as plant and printing presses for manufacturing books. Other costs are variable, which means that they attach to each individual copy. For example, paper, printing, gluing or stitching, inventory maintenance, and shipping are all variable costs.

Still other costs can be either fixed or variable, depending on how they are assessed. For example, if an author gets royalties of 10 percent of sales, that cost would be variable. It goes up or down with the number of sales. However, if the author gets a flat rate up front—say, $100,000 on delivery of the manuscript—then that cost is fixed.

The pricing of a product is driven by its variable (in this case, marginal) costs. The publisher asks: For each additional copy, how much additional net revenue will I earn? When the book in question is an ebook, this calculation is much different than when it is a clothbound or paperback book. Once the computer file for an ebook has been created, the only costs of selling one additional copy are the electronic ones of transmitting the file, customer billing, and the author's royalties, if applicable. The additional copy does not need to be printed, assembled, stored, or shipped (other than electronic transmission). There are no inventory costs, and no costs for retailing through a bookstore.

What this means is that the breakeven price of an ebook is typically much lower than the price of the same title in a traditional hardback or paperback format. Indeed, many ebooks whose copyrights have expired are sold at a price of zero. No royalties are due, and transmission costs are negligible. You can obtain both *Moby-Dick* and *Pride and Prejudice* on Amazon, as well as many other sites, for free. While ebook prices are typically lower than printed book prices for the same title, the price differences that Amazon charges very likely *under*state the cost differences.

As a product, the ebook is differentiated from the traditional book with the same title. What that means is that demand differs. Some people have a strong preference for traditional books. Others prefer ebooks. Others (like this author) buy both, depending on the circumstances. For example, ebooks are good for air travel with a limited amount of luggage space. As a result of differential user preferences, it is unlikely that one technology will drive the other technology from the market, as the digital camera did to the film camera. More likely it will stabilize, if it has not already. Data from 2022 indicate that about 37 percent of readers use printed books exclusively, 28 percent use both, and only 7 percent read digital books exclusively. The market shares measured by copies are roughly 80 percent for printed books and 20 percent for ebooks.[12]

Attempt to Monopolize and "Abuse of Dominance"

The Sherman Antitrust Act prohibits both monopolization and "attempts" to monopolize. The law had long recognized attempt offenses, such as attempted murder. The "attempt" offense is necessary when the conduct was interrupted before the deed was done. In the case of attempted murder, the targeted victim was not successfully killed. An important requirement for attempts is that there be a "dangerous probability of success" in achieving the result. For example, if I attempt to shoot you but my gunpowder is wet, that could be an attempt. You would be dead but for the fortuity of wet powder. However, if I point a banana at you and say "bang," that could not be an attempted murder because no one could foresee a "dangerous probability" of success.

The offense of attempt to monopolize is particularly prone to abuse by competitors who are injured by a larger firm's conduct when the larger firm could not realistically become a monopoly. For example, if I lie to another business about the quality of a computer printer that I am selling, that might be a business tort but not an attempt to monopolize. A successful antitrust plaintiff can get threefold (treble) damages plus attorney fees even for an unsuccessful attempt. So plaintiffs are strongly motivated to turn ordinary business tort claims into antitrust claims.

Businesses frequently engage in conduct that harms their competitors—indeed, to a certain extent that is what competition is about. However, only a small part of this conduct ever leads to a firm's acquisition of a monopoly. One good example of overuse is the *Tops Market* case, which occurred in a very traditional market. Tops was competing with Quality markets to purchase building sites for grocery stores. Tops claimed that Quality interfered with its purchase contracts by continually upping its offers and buying locations out from under Tops. Further, this was part of a pattern that Quality used to keep rivals out of its territory. The court dismissed the monopolization complaint after observing that entry into the grocery business was easy. Undeveloped land was readily available for any number of sites.[13] However, the court continued, proof of an attempt to monopolize requires a "lesser degree" of power, and Tops established this.

The court was effectively condemning the guy with the banana of attempted murder. The point in this case was not merely that Quality's scheme of monopolization failed. Rather, given what the court said about easy entry and widespread availability of sites, it *never* could have succeeded. In that case it could not be monopolization, but it could not be an attempt either.

The approach to monopolization in the United States is narrower than in Europe and some other countries, and in ways that are relevant to big tech. European Union law describes the equivalent offense as "abuse of a dominant position." The difference often shows up when a firm operates in two related markets and has a dominant market share in only one of them. For example, Microsoft continues to have a dominant although declining position in its Windows operating system for desktops and laptops, with a 63 percent market share (2023). Suppose that Windows favors its own web browser, Microsoft Edge, and makes it difficult for Windows users to opt for a different browser. Edge controls only 5 percent of the browser market (2023), so unless something changes dramatically, there is not much chance that Edge will monopolize the market. Currently Google Chrome and Apple Safari are both far larger and dominate small devices, and Mozilla Firefox is a little behind Edge.

Nevertheless, this practice could injure Edge's rivals and Windows customers by making it more difficult to use competing browsers on Windows computers. This conduct could fall within the EU's offense of "abuse of a dominant position." While it may not seriously threaten a browser monopoly, it is an "abuse" that causes harm and that results from Microsoft's dominant position in a complementary market, namely, Windows. By contrast, U.S. antitrust law would condemn this behavior under the Sherman Act only if it threatened monopoly in the browser market.

One antitrust reform worth considering is for U.S. law to adopt the "abuse of dominance" position. It is particularly relevant in networked markets, where a firm with significant power in one market can cause harm in

The approach to monopolization in the United States is narrower than in Europe and some other countries, and in ways that are relevant to big tech.

an interconnected market, but without creating a monopoly there. Apple's use of the iPhone to dominate app purchases is another. For example, Apple's insistence that all game purchases be make through its App Store harmed Epic Games, but there was no realistic possibility that Apple would achieve a monopoly in the gaming market.[14]

Anticompetitive Agreements and Default Rules

Exclusive and preferential agreements have always been a focus of antitrust policy. A few, including naked price fixing, market division, and boycotts, are unlawful "per se," without proof of market power. Joint ventures that include significant joint innovation, production, or distribution are treated under the rule of reason. Nearly all purely vertical agreements are also examined under the rule of reason. Such agreements can be either beneficial or harmful, depending on the presence of market power and anticompetitive effects.

So far, relatively few anticompetitive horizontal agreements involving big tech have come to light. One important one was the Apple/book publishers' cartel, designed to keep eBook prices high. The late Steve Jobs, then head of Apple, had developed the iPad and wanted it to be linked to Apple's own Bookstore. However, Jobs believed that Amazon's ebook prices were too low for Apple's own entry to be profitable. He got the major book publishers to agree to fix the prices of ebooks and impose these higher prices on Amazon. With Amazon's prices raised, it would be easier for Apple to enter the ebook market. The government sued the publishers and Apple. The publishers, who had unwisely created a thick email record confirming their guilt, quickly settled. Apple litigated and eventually lost in a federal court of appeals. Some people defended Apple, arguing that Amazon's book prices were too low. As noted before, however, the price of ebooks was lower than the price of traditional books because of the structural differences between the two products.

Several big tech antitrust complaints have involved vertical agreements that exclude rivals or raise their costs. For example, "most favored nation" (MFN) agreements require one party to "favor" it over rivals. Amazon has used contracts with merchants that forbade them from selling the same product at a materially lower price through a different seller. An FTC complaint filed against Amazon in September 2023, accuses it of demoting sellers' product rankings if the good in question is sold at a lower price on another site.

MFNs are not inherently anticompetitive. For example, a contractor bidding on a construction job needs assurance that its bid will be competitive. One possibility is a contract provision that guarantees that if a supplier sells the product to someone else at a lower price, the seller will match the discount to this contractor as well. However, MFNs can also be a way for dominant firms to protect their positions from competition. These different possibilities mean that MFN clauses are treated under the rule of reason, which requires proof of anticompetitive effects.

Restraints on product differentiation are more suspicious. These restraints make it more difficult for a competitor to distinguish itself from the dominant firm imposing the restraint. Most dominant tech firms do not need to worry very much about new competition from clones. For example, a firm that simply copied all of Facebook's features, with perhaps some name changes to avoid trademark problems, would almost certainly fail. Facebook simply has too big a head start. That is why the successful new firms that compete with Facebook have different features, including Instagram before Meta purchased it, X (formerly Twitter), and TikTok.

The problem facing dominant tech companies is *differentiated* entry. A restraint on differentiation effectively tells a contracting partner that any new feature it or one of its customers develops must be licensed to and capable of being copied by the dominant firm.[15] At this writing some restrictions of this type have been condemned under European law, although not in the United States.

One type of vertical agreement that digital networking has made prominent is tying agreements, under which someone can purchase one product or service only in combination with a second one. Chapter 1 briefly traced their history. Ties are extremely common in tech markets, depending on how "tie" is defined. For example, an iPhone comes with both Apple's operating system and its App Store preinstalled. Facebook automatically includes a large number of features. While you don't have to use all of them, you cannot get a version of Facebook that excludes the ones you don't want. Anyone who installs a new version of the Microsoft Windows operating system automatically gets Microsoft's Edge browser. A subscription to Amazon Prime automatically covers physical products, music, and movies. A customer cannot force Amazon to sell a lower-priced version of Prime that covers, say, only ebooks. Neither can you subscribe to a version of Netflix that provides only westerns or Tom Cruise movies. Office suites such as Microsoft Office include at least a word processing program, an email program, a database, and a spreadsheet. Once someone purchases such a suite she has much less incentive to purchase one of these programs separately elsewhere. While the seller may offer individual items separately, the price is higher, and the law of tying covers discounts as well as absolute tying requirements.

As these illustrations suggest, some ties are created by a contract or agreement that requires two or more products to be purchased together. For example, the Supreme Court once held that someone who obtained surgery at a hospital could be required to use that hospital's own approved anesthesiologists.[16] In high tech, however, many ties are accomplished by technological design rather than by an agreement. For example, the App Store is preinstalled on a new iPhone, and users cannot delete it. Windows 10 or 11 comes with the Microsoft Edge browser and its Bing search engine preinstalled as defaults. We generally refer to these as technological ties, or "tech ties." Courts usually treat them as "unilateral" acts of design rather than agreement. As a result, they can be addressed only under section 2 of the Sherman Act, with its higher market power requirements.

As these illustrations suggest, tying arrangements are not inherently bad. Most are beneficial, or at least harmless, and particularly for digital products. In fact, a great deal of innovation consists in combining products that were previously separate. Nevertheless, purchasing products in a bundle can make it harder for sellers of individual products to compete. Even computer hardware is a "tie" of its constituent parts. For example, if you purchase a desktop or laptop it will almost certainly have a hard drive, memory chips, and other operating components preinstalled. For a laptop this even includes the keyboard and screen. This contrasts with the way computers were sold in the 1970s and earlier, when these individual pieces were separate devices connected by cables. At the time, IBM successfully defeated antitrust claims that its consolidation of many computer parts into the single box that eventually became the personal computer amounted to anticompetitive tying.[17]

In other situations, such as digital streaming, transaction costs justify putting everything into one bundle. One antitrust case rejected a demand by the Triple Nickel bar for a reduced price on a music licensing package that included only country and western music. A contract limited to "Country & Western," as the Triple Nickel wanted for its jukebox, could invite disputes about coverage, such as whether Elvis or Taylor Swift belonged in the bundle. Further, since the cost of electronic transmission is virtually zero, it costs no less to transmit or license a subset than for the entire database. The court in the *Triple Nickel* case found that the costs of slicing up digital agreements by genre would actually be higher than the costs of simply giving everyone the entire package.[18]

Innovation often involves a process of combining two things into a single unit. For example, horses and buggies used to be sold separately, but the automobile and its engine came to be sold as a single unit. Should we make this change unlawful? Most of us lack the skills to buy a car body and install our own engines. The original operating systems for desktop computers did little more than operate the disks, requiring all software to be loaded separately. By contrast, a modern operating system such as Windows or the Mac OS is a conglomeration of separate features, and computer makers often add still more. Many of these additions harm rivals in the market for the added product. They must now compete with an effective price of zero. For example, Microsoft's preinstallation of a solitaire game harms the independent market for computer games. Cameras and film used to be separate products, but the digital camera is a single product that includes both. Speaking of separable cameras and film is not even meaningful. Today, smartphones and cameras are also tied into a single unit. While a user can disable the camera, she cannot buy a new iPhone without one. One result is that sales of dedicated digital cameras have declined to about 10 percent of what they were ten years ago. Should camera makers be able to challenge this phone-camera tie as an antitrust violation? Overwhelmingly, tying that included cameras on smartphones achieved (virtually) universal acceptance because that is what customers wanted.

Many of these ties are nonexclusive in the sense that the user is free to add additional secondary products. While you as a user cannot remove Bing from Windows, you can add additional search engines of your own, ignoring the preinstalled ones. So the main thing that the tie does in this case is give the dominant seller's own tied product a startup advantage. That may or may not be significant.

In other cases, such as IBM's development of the personal computer, a key to making computers faster, smaller, and cheaper was preinstallation of the components into the same box. Back in the 1940s, Supreme Court justice

Innovation often involves a process of combining two things into a single unit.

Felix Frankfurter declared that "tying arrangements serve hardly any purpose beyond the suppression of competition."[19] Today that statement seems wildly off-base. In 1979 a court held that IBM's collapsing of many parts of the computer into a single box was not simple "technological manipulation" but introduction of an improved product.[20]

Nevertheless, some ties are unnecessarily restrictive. One likely example is Apple's insistence that users of its iPhone purchase all their apps through iPhone's App Store. Most Android cell phones assess a similar requirement through Google Play. As a result, the software-buying process on a handheld device is much more restrictive than the one that occurs on a desktop or laptop, where users can purchase from any software seller with a website.

As noted earlier, Epic Games lost its antitrust challenge to Apple's practice of requiring all app purchases for the iPhone to be made through its App Store. Although 100 percent of software purchased for the iPhone had to come through the App Store, the iPhone itself accounted for less than half of the smartphone market. Further, Epic's games can be played on numerous other devices, including desktops, laptops, and dedicated game players. If all these were grouped together, the market share controlled by Apple was in fact quite small.

The question posed by *Epic Games* is fundamental. Should market power in such a case be measured only over the range of iPhone users, which would give iPhone 100 percent of app purchases? Or should it be measured across the full range of platforms that use a particular app, even though switching among them is sometimes costly? The technical econometric tools that we use typically find significant market power in such settings, particularly where switching costs are high. For example, in the case of the iPhone, one can avoid Apple's App Store only by switching to a different phone.

A closely related area of exclusivity or bias is default rules. A default is something that is done a certain way to begin with, but a user may change it. For example, Google Search is preinstalled as the default search engine on most smartphones. If you purchase an iPhone, it comes with Safari as its default web browser. However, any user who wishes can add additional search engines or browsers, and even change the default. The app stores on both Androids and iPhones make several available.

Consider two defaults involving the same product, Google Search. Someone who purchases a new desktop or laptop with Microsoft Windows installed automatically gets Bing, a Microsoft product, as her default search engine. A very high percentage of these customers reject the default and switch to Google Search. By contrast, someone who purchases either an Android phone or an iPhone in the United States (as of 2023) gets Google Search as the default search engine. A very small percentage of customers switch. Why the big difference?

One possibility is that defaults are "stickier" on hand-held devices than they are on larger computers. Another is that customers widely regard Google Search as superior to alternatives, so they readily switch *toward* Google Search but not away from it. Alphabet, the owner of Google Search, pays Apple several billion dollars annually for its default status on the iPhone. If switching were actually easy and costless, making Google Search the default would not be very valuable.

If a practice is just a suggestion or recommendation, or falls short of absolute insistence, it is not unlawful tying under established antitrust law. The tougher question is whether it can be condemned as a form of monopolization when it is imposed by a dominant firm. Here the behavioral evidence can be helpful. How many customers would switch if switching costs were lower? How big a burden are defaults for firms that are not the default choice? At this writing, the government is challenging the Google Search defaults in a widely watched trial in Washington, DC, regarding this very issue.

The debate over defaults often reduces to a dispute between "neoclassical" and "behavioral" approaches to consumer choice. According to neoclassical economics, consumers have a rational set of preferences and will switch as long as long as the costs of switching are less than the expected gains. By contrast, behavioral economics takes a more empirical approach, focusing on the choices that consumers actually make and that often cannot be so rationally explained. Notably, the behavioral approach tends to find competitive harm more frequently.

Anticompetitive Tech Mergers

Many big tech companies are serial acquirers. Wikipedia maintains lists of all the firms acquired by major platforms, numbering in the hundreds. Some are quite large. These include Amazon's acquisitions of Whole Foods and MGM, Alphabet's purchase of Motorola Mobility and YouTube, and Apple's acquisitions of Beats and Intel Smartphone. The lists also include hundreds of small acquisitions, including some with only a handful of employees and some that have not even made their first sale. The merger laws require that mergers above a certain size be reported to the antitrust agencies. Many of these mergers are too small to require reporting.

What is the point of all these mergers? Many involve the integration of a new technology, patents or copyrights, or new talent that enables the platform to perform better or be more attractive to its customers. For most, the acquisition of physical assets is a relatively minor factor. That is, Facebook did not purchase Instagram or WhatsApp because it wanted their buildings or computer hardware. In a small minority of platform acquisitions the value lies in the acquired firm's physical assets. One example is Amazon's non-tech acquisition of Whole Foods and its roughly 500 stores. That was an attempt to facilitate Amazon's entry into the higher-end grocery business.

Historically, the dominant reason that we have an antitrust policy controlling mergers is the fear of higher prices. For example, a "horizontal" merger of competitors reduces by one the number of firms in a market. If a market has 100 competitors, this will not have much of an impact. But if a merger takes a market from, say, five firms to four, then the risk of collusion or oligopoly increases. When that happens, prices in the entire market tend to rise.

Other mergers are challenged because they enable the merging firms to increase their prices, although the prices of other firms in the market typically do not change. This occurs when the market's products are differentiated and the merging firms are "close" to one another in the product space. For example, suppose the automobile market has ten firms but two of them, Mercedes and BMW, make luxury cars and are particularly close competitors to each other. Other firms, such as Toyota, GM, or Ford, compete too, but not so closely. In that case a merger of Mercedes and BMW might eliminate the strongest rival for each of those firms. The merged company will be able to increase prices in the luxury portion of the market, but with a relatively small effect on other firms. Such mergers are called "unilateral effects" mergers because only the merging firm is likely to increase its price significantly. Today, many merger challenges in markets for differentiated products fall into this category.

Some big tech acquisitions do not belong in either of these categories. Rather, the purpose or effect of the merger is to eliminate a potential rival before it has a chance to grow into a more formidable competitor. In fact, using mergers to eliminate threats from *potential* competitors is very likely an important reason why the big tech firms have been able to maintain their dominant positions. Here, the FTC's complaint against Meta (Facebook), which is pending at this writing, is a welcome change. The complaint recites how apprehensive Facebook's managers were that WhatsApp and Instagram would grow into large and formidable competitors with Facebook, so it purchased them instead.

This problem is a real one, but it does create a dilemma. On the one hand, these firms offer features that could make Facebook more valuable to its customers. On the other, they might develop into formidable rivals. How can we preserve the benefits created by the first alternative without risking the anticompetitive threat?

One possibility is to permit Meta to acquire *non*exclusive licenses to Instagram's or WhatsApp's patents, copyrights, and other IP. A nonexclusive right usually gives a firm everything it needs to improve its own technology but not to exclude someone else. For example, when you subscribe to a streaming service such as Spotify (music) or MAX (formerly HBO+, movies), you obtain *non*exclusive rights. You can listen or watch as much as your agreement permits. What you cannot do, however, is interfere with anyone else's right to do the same thing. A nonexclusive license to WhatsApp's IP would give Meta everything it needed to incorporate WhatsApp's distinctive features into its own technology. However, WhatsApp would still be around as an independent company, able either to operate or else to give other firms nonexclusive rights.

One objection to this limitation is that the price of a nonexclusive license would be much lower than the price of an outright purchase of WhatsApp. That might be true, but is it a legitimate objection? A merger such as this has two different effects. One is the "integration" effect, which is the ability to improve one's own product. This is the reason we permit many mergers. The other is the "exclusion" effect, which is the ability to prevent others from having access. The thrust of a nonexclusive license remedy is that we permit these mergers for their integrative effects but not for their exclusion effects. Challenging a merger on this basis should require proof of a serious risk of an exclusion effect. If that can be shown, then the purchasing firm should be limited to a nonexclusive license.[21] If talent is what it is after, it can always hire the talent.

This reasoning also indicates why "killer" acquisitions can be harmful. In a killer acquisition a firm acquires another firm only to shut down all or a significant portion of its operations. Killer acquisitions are well known in the history of antitrust laws. Already in the 1911 *American Tobacco* case the defendant acquired its position by purchasing rivals and shutting them down, removing their plants from the market. Such an acquisition has no integrative benefits because no integration is occurring. As a result, none of the efficiency benefits of mergers will ever materialize. Its only value is exclusionary—in this case, to keep potential rivals out of the market.[22]

Conclusion

Identifying and then addressing anticompetitive practices by large tech firms is not easy. First, many of the practices are ambiguous: both pro-competitive and anticompetitive explanations are plausible. Second, the firms themselves are complex, and often courts must determine how a practice fits into the firm's overall operations. Third, economic growth in big tech has been significantly higher than in the economy overall. We should be cautious before wading into big tech markets with a machete to hack them down to size. Antitrust's purpose is not to hobble the economy for the benefit of those who compete with big tech firms, particularly if consumers and labor suffer in the process. Nevertheless, it also seems clear that big tech firms are doing anticompetitive things. Markets would be more competitive if these were addressed. In the vast majority of cases the effective remedy will be an injunction, not a breakup.

This is in fact a very old story in the history of antitrust. In its early years, antitrust enforcers confronted such firms as Standard Oil, American Can, and United States Steel. Progressives of that day painted a one-dimensional picture of these firms as doing nothing but engaging in anticompetitive actions with the intent to destroy competition. A little later, people on the right painted a sharply contrasting picture of these firms as highly innovative risk-takers that did nothing but attempt to increase their own output by pleasing customers. Eventually, as the truth emerged, it lay between. Firms are inherently self-interested, motivated by profit, and profits can come from both innovation and anticompetitive exclusion. We can fully expect them to take advantage of both. Over the course of history, they have done so. This gives antitrust policy the difficult task of distinguishing them.

ANTITRUST SOLUTIONS TO TECH MONOPOLY PROBLEMS

Once the legal system has found an antitrust violation, it must create a remedy. This is where antitrust cases often falter. Finding a violation is often easier than figuring out how to fix it. In *Microsoft*, a tech monopoly case discussed earlier, the court described an ideal remedy, drawing from several Supreme Court decisions:

> A remedies decree in an antitrust case must seek to [1] "unfetter a market from anticompetitive conduct," to [2] "terminate the illegal monopoly, [3] deny to the defendant the fruits of its statutory violation, and [4] ensure that there remain no practices likely to result in monopolization in the future. . . ."[1]

That is a tall order. Few antitrust remedies have accomplished all of these things. That includes the *Microsoft* decision itself. Many people at the time thought that the remedy was too weak because it did not break up any part of Microsoft, leaving both its Internet Explorer (IE) browser and Microsoft Office Suite of productivity programs intact.

Today, however, the structure of that market has changed remarkably. Microsoft remains dominant in the desktop/laptop operating system market, where Windows has a share of around 64 percent and Apple's Mac OS around 18 percent. Microsoft's share of the internet browser market has plummeted to below 5 percent, significantly lower than Google Chrome (64 percent). Further, these market shares fluctuate significantly from year to year, suggesting a high degree of competition. Both the iPhone (introduced in 2007) and Android phone (introduced in 2008), which took substantial usage away from traditional computers, were several years in the future. Search engines played almost no part in the *Microsoft* decision, even though Google Search and Alta Vista already existed. Today search is dominated by Google, and Microsoft's own product, Bing, has about 3 percent of the market.

How many of these changes resulted from the court's decree and how many from other things, such as Google's dramatic rise, Apple's expansion, or the introduction of smartphones? There is no conclusive answer. One thing the market share data suggest, however, is that a court need not "break up" a firm in order to correct its

Once the legal system has found an antitrust violation, it must create a remedy. This is where antitrust cases often falter.

anticompetitive behavior. Microsoft had attempted to protect its IE browser share with an array of exclusive agreements linking IE to Windows. The court issued injunctions against most of these, and in later years the browser market became much more competitive. At the very least, the injunctions freed up the market, permitting competitive innovation to run its course.

What should a good antitrust remedy do? First and foremost, it must address the problem, which requires an understanding of whom the antitrust defendant is harming and how. Undoing that and seeing that it will not occur again is the main purpose of a good remedy. Second, the remedy should not do too much collateral damage. For example, simply destroying a firm may ensure that it will not behave anticompetitively in the future, but neither will it benefit the economy or do the public any good. It also harms largely innocent stockholders, employees, and others whose livelihoods depend on that firm. Ideally, the remedy should be some kind of rehabilitation that enables the firm to continue in a productive role, except more competitively. This is particularly important when the firm has been highly successful. In retrospect, the remedy in *Microsoft* may not have been so bad after all.

The remedy provisions in the antitrust laws give the federal courts a great deal of power, but they are severely lacking in detail.[2] For example, the provision that governs most Justice Department suits authorizes the Antitrust Division to "prevent and restrain" antitrust violations. What particular penalties will accomplish this is left entirely up to the courts.

Both the Justice Department and the Federal Trade Commission (FTC) have broad authority to condemn antitrust violations without showing causation of any particular harm. By contrast, while private persons can enforce the antitrust laws, they must show that they suffered actual or threatened harm as a result of the antitrust violation. Actual harm is based on past conduct, and the ordinary remedy is treble (threefold) damages. Threatened harm is feared in the future, and the usual remedy is an injunction against the threatening conduct.

These differing requirements for public and private enforcers are hardly unique to antitrust. The legal system applies them in many types of criminal and tort law. For example, a police officer can write a ticket for speeding or drunk driving even though the driver has not had an accident and did not hurt anyone. The police officer's function is risk management, which requires preventing likely harm before it occurs. The legal system does not give private citizens a roving mandate to punish speeders or drunk drivers, however. They can sue if they or their property have been injured in an accident. The same logic applies to private enforcement of the antitrust laws.

Remedies and Causation

The difference between public and private enforcers can be important when causation is difficult to prove. This is a common problem in cases involving innovation. In *Microsoft*, the court had little difficulty concluding in the government's suit that Microsoft violated the Sherman Act by pressuring Intel to stop development of a "multiplatform" processor chip. The chip would have increased compatibility between Microsoft and non-Microsoft products by permitting code to be translated between them more quickly.[3] Microsoft feared that if compatibility were increased, users could more easily switch away from Windows or the Internet Explorer browser and use competitors' products. It would be better for Microsoft to ensure that its own products remained incompatible with those of competitors.

A few years later, however, a court rejected a private antitrust suit by computer users challenging exactly the same conduct. In order to prove their harm, the court held, the plaintiffs would have to show that the multiplatform chip project would have succeeded had it continued, how many people would have taken advantage of it, and how increased interoperability would have benefited each user. These things would very likely be impossible to prove. "At bottom," the court concluded, "the harms that the plaintiffs have alleged with respect to the loss of competitive technologies are so diffuse that they could not possibly be adequately measured."

This story reveals an important dilemma that antitrust policy faces in highly innovative markets. As economists often say, innovation is "badly behaved." At the beginning of any project there is often no way of telling whether it will succeed and, if so, how successful it will be, how many people will adopt it, and how much better off they will be as a result. These things may be easier to determine after the innovation has entered the market successfully, but anticompetitive restraints on innovation target innovations before they have a chance to emerge, as in the *Microsoft* case. This suggests that public enforcers should have a bigger role to play when conduct threatens to restrain innovation before it is developed, but prediction of effects is almost impossible. At the same time, maintaining enforcement in this area is doubly important because innovation contributes much more to economic growth than does competition under static technology. A corollary is that restraints on innovation can do significantly more harm than simple restraints on price competition.

When the antitrust violation is a more traditional anticompetitive agreement, such as those discussed in chapter 3, injured firms are often better able to provide a reasonable estimate of the harm. For example, people who pay higher prices to a cartel, or firms that lose business because of anticompetitive exclusion, typically have measurable harm. Proof of such injuries often requires expert testimony, but estimating it is well within the realm of possibility.

Injunctions and Damages

The *Microsoft* decision also held that an antitrust remedy should attempt to "restore competitive conditions." For example, if the result of an antitrust violation is to reduce market output and increase price, then the remedy should be at least a reasonable attempt to restore price competition. In some cases, such as unlawful mergers, the best remedy may be divestiture, or undoing of the unlawful acquisition. In cases involving enforcement of anticompetitive agreements, such as exclusive contracts or most favored nation (MFN) provisions, the best remedy may be a simple injunction that prohibits enforcement of the practice, plus damages for harm already done.

Of all antitrust remedies, injunctions against repetition of unlawful conduct have the best track record, are the easiest to design, and typically are the easiest to enforce. If properly designed, they also do less collateral damage. This hardly means they are perfect. One frequent complaint about injunctions is that they can be too little, too late. For example, if Google Search or Meta has already acquired a dominant position by means of an anticompetitive practice, a simple injunction prohibiting that practice may not be sufficient to restore competitive conditions. Perhaps it will do no more than maintain the status quo.

The android/Google Search remedy imposed by the European Commission, which enforces EU competition law, has provoked this complaint. Alphabet (Google) owns both the Android operating system for cellular phones and Google Search, which is the world's market-dominant search engine. For years, Alphabet made Google Search the default search engine on Android devices. As noted in chapter 3, customers can switch away from a default system, but most small device owners do not do so. Rival search engines complained that this default rule gave Alphabet a big advantage in search engine choice on cellular phones, and in 2020 it settled an antitrust complaint by agreeing to a "choice screen," such as the one shown in figure 6 for Android devices sold in the EU.

This screen entitled purchasers of a new Android phone to select their default search engine. The intent was to create a more neutral playing field among several options. As of this writing the United States does not have this rule. Competitors such as Microsoft, whose search engine is Bing, and independent search engines such as DuckDuckGo have complained that simply opening up competition after Google had already obtained 90+ percent of the market was not adequate. Indeed, since choice

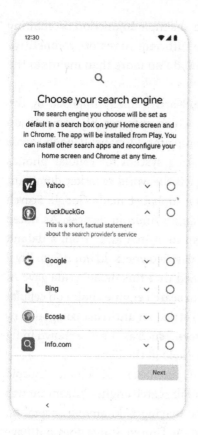

Figure 6

came into effect, Google Search's European share on Android devices has barely changed. Google claims this is because it has a more desirable search engine, while rivals say that it reflects prior embedded biases in favor of Google Search.[4]

Some injunctions can be difficult to administer. For example, suppose the defendant is condemned for predatory pricing, or charging a below-cost price in order to exclude competitors. We could order the defendant to increase its price, but to what level? A court needs a great deal of confidence that it has identified predatory pricing correctly before it forces a higher price as part of an antitrust remedy. Further, how should we determine such a price if costs continuously change? In that case the antitrust remedy simply becomes become price regulation by another name, and courts are notoriously bad at that.

Other injunctions against anticompetitive practices are easier to enforce and more effective. For example, most of the remedies in *Microsoft* were injunctions against agreements found to be anticompetitive, and many appear to have succeeded. The anticompetitive agreements included Microsoft's insistence that internet access providers and applications developers use Internet Explorer exclusively as their browser, and the pressure Microsoft placed on Apple to use IE as its default browser. With that pressure removed, Apple then developed Safari, which it introduced in 2003 as its own internet browser. Netscape as an entity never recovered from Microsoft's conduct. After the court's decision, however, Mozilla Firefox acquired and used Netscape's code, and Google Chrome emerged, along with others as new browsers.

In retrospect, the court's order prohibiting Microsoft from excluding competing Microsoft browsers appears to have succeeded. These types of remedies, it should be noted, work better in innovative, fast-moving markets, where the injunction serves mainly to open up opportunities. The Microsoft injunctions very largely opened the door for Google.

Antitrust damages are intended for private plaintiffs, although the government can obtain them when it is suing for its own injuries, such as when it purchases goods or services for federal agencies or the military. Damages are trebled by law, and the defendant must also pay a winning plaintiff's attorneys' fees. Damages are charged both to compensate injured parties, as the private legal system has always done, and also to deter unlawful conduct. They are important because the vast majority of antitrust complaints are private. Most of these include demands for treble damages.

Antitrust damages come in two kinds. "Lost profits" are most generally given to businesses that were injured as competitors of the defendant, or which lost business opportunities as a result of an antitrust violation. By contrast, "overcharge" damages occur when a consumer or other party overpays because of unlawful monopoly or cartel prices. In 2019 the Supreme Court held that consumers who purchased apps through their iPhones and overpaid because of an antitrust violation could obtain damages.[5] The alleged violation was Apple's insistence that all app purchases on iPhones be made through Apple's own App Store, thus eliminating competition within the iPhone platform itself. For those sales, Apple was charging a very high commission that was being challenged as monopolistic.

Structural Remedies—"Breakups"

A common misconception is that antitrust is routinely in the business of breaking up big firms. Actually, very few antitrust cases end up in structural breakups. For one thing, the courts do not have an admirable track record. For example, the government's early (1911) case against John D. Rockefeller's Standard Oil Company broke up that firm into thirty-four companies. Immediately the price of gasoline shot up, forcing an embarrassed Federal Trade Commission to write a multivolume report explaining how that could have happened.[6] Should increased competition lead to higher prices? The cure should not be worse than the disease.

The law of mergers invites some confusion about breakups. Early merger enforcement involved challenges to completed mergers. The most common remedy was the undoing of the merger, or spinning off of the acquired companies or assets. The merger law makes it unlawful to acquire another firm when competitive harm is likely. The preferred remedy simply reverses the unlawful acquisition. In 1976, however, Congress passed legislation that requires the parties to report significant mergers in advance. That law gave the Justice Department and the FTC a window to evaluate the proposed merger and, if appropriate, sue for an injunction to prevent it. This can be a far less disruptive remedy than spinning off assets that may already have been integrated into the parent company's operations. Today most mergers are challenged before they occur.

Even post-acquisition spin-offs need not be particularly disruptive, however. Depending on the assets and the technology, integrating an acquired firm into the parent's business often takes a long time and sometimes never happens at all. For example, Facebook acquired Instagram in 2012 and WhatsApp in 2014. At this writing, however, the two firms have not disappeared into the structure of Meta. An order requiring them to be spun off, as the FTC is requesting in ongoing antitrust litigation, is likely to be much less disruptive than an order breaking up facilities or features that were internally developed. Likewise, Alphabet (Google) acquired YouTube in 2006, and YouTube continues to have its own distinct website and customer base. Forcing Alphabet to sell YouTube may not be all that difficult. Such a spin-off poses a different problem, however: it may not make any market more competitive. A forced spin-off of YouTube may simply transfer a near monopoly (with a 76 percent video market share in 2022) to a different owner, leaving its market share unaffected.

In other cases, acquired assets are completely submerged into the acquiring firm's business. This is particularly true when the acquired firm offers a feature that the parent incorporates into its own technology. For example, Alphabet acquired Viewdle in 2012 in order to improve its ability to do image searches on Android. Once incorporated, Viewdle simply became another integrated part of the Android operating system.

An alternative to spin-offs exists that can often preserve many of the advantages of the merger but without the competitive harm. If the acquired firm's assets are principally patents or copyrights, as they often are in high tech, the firm could be permitted to acquire only a nonexclusive license, leaving the target company intact and able to continue in business on its own or license to others. The nonexclusive license, discussed in the previous chapter, will not work in every situation. When it does, however, it can give the acquiring firm everything it needs to improve its own business, but not the power to eliminate competition.

Breaking *into* the Monopoly

One important principle for antitrust breakups is that if monopoly is the problem, the breakup must promise a solution. Courts have made an important error here in imposing remedies that do not break up the monopoly. For example, if we have identified Google Search as a problematic monopoly, then simply forcing Alphabet to sell it to someone else may not solve anything. All that will do is transfer the monopoly to a different owner, which will go right on dominating the market. An effective remedy must break *into* the monopoly. This is more easily said than done.

Suppose that a maker of small appliances controls 80 percent of the market's toasters, 50 percent of its blenders, and 35 percent of its electric mixers. A "breakup" that forces this firm to sell its toaster division will simply give us one firm that makes 80 percent of the market's toasters and another firm that makes 50 percent of its blenders and 35 percent of its mixers. To break up the monopoly, we need to break *into* the toaster business. That kind of breakup can be far more disruptive. For example, toasters and other appliances require different assembly lines and parts. They may even be made in different plants. Breaking into the monopoly would require dividing toaster production and sharing it among two or more owners. That may require construction of a new plant, although perhaps not. If the firm is currently making toasters in two or more different plants, divesting one of them might be relatively simple.

Digital technologies such as Google Search or Facebook proper typically do not lend themselves to the kind of breakup that would actually make the market more competitive. Breaking into Facebook might occur if we, say, created one platform for users in the Northern Hemisphere and another for users in the Southern Hemisphere, or one for men and another for women, or else forced it to abandon one or more features, such as video posting. The principal thing these breakups would accomplish would be to make Facebook less valuable for everyone, including its users. Breaking up Google Search would be even more difficult.

In a few cases, spinning off a monopoly asset may be justified because we can predict competition down the road. For example, even if Google Search remained a monopoly after a spin-off, a separately owned Google Search might begin looking for competitive opportunities. This could include increased competition with its former parent company. At the same time, the parent company might develop a new search engine to compete with Google Search. These are always possibilities, but we need to be cautious about trading off immediate losses in operating effectiveness or consumer benefit in exchange for the mere promise of more competition in the future.

One sobering bit of history is the antitrust telephone breakup that divided the AT&T system into seven regional operating companies (the "Baby Bells"). Each of these continued to have a monopoly of local calling in its service area. Enforcers hoped each firm would expand into the service areas controlled by the others, although doing so as a competitor. Twenty years later, however, not a single one had expanded.[7] What did happen is that the original AT&T merged with two of the Baby Bells, and two other Baby Bells merged together to form Verizon.

Most of the increased competition that did occur after the *AT&T* decree came not from territorial expansion in traditional service but rather from new technologies, including wireless. The reason the AT&T breakup succeeded was not because of these geographic divisions but rather because of its interconnection requirements with others. These are discussed later in this chapter.

Remedies and "Winner-Take-All" Markets

The term "winner-take-all" applies in situations in which a single firm is likely to take over the entire market. The economic term is "natural monopoly" because in such markets, production tends to gravitate toward a single firm. The classic example is a water or gas line. For any given volume of water, it is always cheaper to run a single larger line than two smaller ones. A three-inch pipe will carry more than twice as much water as a two-inch pipe and costs much less than putting in two two-inch pipes. As a result, services such as water, natural gas, or electricity are usually supplied to a home or business by a single provider, whose price is typically regulated. In most situations running two water lines into a building in order to have "competition" would actually yield higher prices because the increased cost of constructing and operating two lines would make competitive provision more costly.

Network effects can also create winner-take-all situations because many of them become more valuable as they grow. For example, a larger number of drivers on a ride-hailing network such as Uber will attract more passengers, which will in turn attract yet more drivers, and so on. A bigger ride-hailing network will have advantages over a smaller one.

The classic example of a winner-take-all network is the phone company. It becomes more valuable as the number of users becomes larger. Further, this effect continues right up to the point that the entire market is exhausted. The optimal number of telephone networks worldwide is one, in which everyone can be on the network with everyone else. That comes close to the phone system that we actually have: users employing a variety of wired and wireless technologies located all around the world are able to communicate with each other. That result, obtained by the "interoperability" portion of the *AT&T* decree, counts as one of antitrust law's most successful remedies.

Winner-take-all markets pose special problems for breakups because we do not want to divide a natural monopoly market into multiple pieces. For example, no one would favor a court decree that broke the telephone network into five geographic networks where people in one network could talk only to others on the same network. One important implication is that breakup remedies should generally not divide up networks.

Most networks are not winner-take-all, however, for one simple reason: product differentiation. The theory of natural monopoly traditionally focused on markets such as electricity or water lines in which the firms sold exactly the same product and competed on price. In that situation, the fact that costs declined as the firm became larger guaranteed that larger firms would knock out smaller ones until the market reached monopoly. All you needed to know is that the cost of delivering water through a single larger line is less than the cost of using two smaller ones.

Product differentiation upends this calculus because the firms no longer compete strictly on price. Once they can realistically compete on other features, all bets are off. Consider, for example, the market for internet dating, which is subject to strong indirect network effects. The "seekers" on a dating site generally prefer one that has a larger number of "sought," or potential dating partners, and vice versa. So why isn't the online dating industry just like the phone system, with everyone on the same network and able to connect with everyone else?

The reason is that people value specialization when it eases searching and engaging with others. Dating sites include Match.com, a fairly traditional site; AdultFriend-Finder for more casual hookups; eHarmony, which caters to older people; JDate for Jewish people; Christian Mingle for evangelicals; SingleParentMeet for single parents; PURRsonals for cat lovers; and the list goes on. In 2021 the United States alone had some 2,500 dating sites. Many of these will undoubtedly fail, but every competitively structured market is a revolving door of firms coming in and out. So in the case of online dating, it appears that the value of product differentiation overwhelms network effects.

Subscription magazines and newspapers are similar. A large subscriber base attracts more advertisers, and advertising revenue helps reduce subscription prices. Offsetting this, however, is considerable product differentiation. For example, *Teen Vogue* and *Field & Stream* have roughly equal numbers of subscribers, but they have very few of the *same* subscribers or advertisers. So network effects extend within a particular demographic, not across different ones. Indeed, the sad story of newspapers in the United States is that winner-take-all outlets often dominated because they could not differentiate themselves sufficiently, or else the differentiations were readily copied. For example, once a paper offers both conservative and liberal columnists, there is less reason to subscribe to one as opposed to another. Many cities have moved from multiple newspapers to just one or two.

The FTC considered product differentiation in its 2021 antitrust complaint against Facebook. It claimed that new entrants into competition with Facebook would be different from Facebook itself. That is, a firm that attempted to enter the market with an exact Facebook clone would almost certainly fail. Unless Facebook took a serious stumble, a simple clone would never be able to compete with Facebook's enormous installed base of users with their built-up histories, advertisers, and features.

In fact, several firms have entered successfully into competition with Facebook. These include Instagram, which Facebook gobbled up, but also X (Twitter), TikTok, Reddit, and others. Each of these differs from its competitors, however, and appeals to different but overlapping groups of users. Indeed, some of them operate as both complements and substitutes—that is, some users as well as advertisers participate in more than one site. Differentiation from Facebook is not difficult because the format and features of a social network site are variable across a wide range. They appeal to users with different tastes.

For other digital platforms, however, meaningful product differentiation is difficult to achieve. These are more likely to be winner-take-all markets. One likely candidate is consumer search. Other than improving the quality of search results, there are not many ways in which search engine providers can meaningfully distinguish their products. For a time, DuckDuckGo offered search confidentiality as a unique feature, but today most of the major search engines also permit "stealth" or "incognito" searching. That itself is part of an old and well understood practice: firms try to succeed by differentiating their products, but established firms then copy the successful differentiations. The difficulty of differentiating search engines in a durable way may explain why Alphabet's Google Search has been able to control around 90 percent of the search engine market, notwithstanding very low switching costs. As of 2023, no rival has more than 3 percent.

Assuming that Google Search is a winner-take-all product, that should also tell us something about effective antitrust remedies. First of all, an order either spinning Google Search off as a free-standing firm or transferring it to a different owner is not likely to solve any monopoly problems, at least in the short term. It will simply assign the monopoly to a different owner. Second, there is very likely no nondisastrous way of "breaking up" Google search into two or more pieces, just as there is no harmless way of breaking up the phone company into mutually exclusive networks.

To be sure, this may not settle the spin-off question entirely. For example, Alphabet, Google's parent company, owns Google Search, Android, YouTube, Waymo (for autonomous vehicles), and some other assets. It is possible that spinning off Google Search could address some other competitive problems resulting from the fact that

Alphabet owns so many businesses that may have a connection to Google Search.

That may be so, but we must be cautious. First, there may be better solutions to the problem. For example, Google Search is the default search engine on Android phones sold in the United States, and that gives it a competitive advantage. However, there is no necessary connection between common ownership of the two technologies and the default status. As noted above, the EU has already attempted to address this problem by requiring Android to provide a choice screen for the default search engine. Further, Google Search at this writing is also the default search engine on Apple iPhones, which are not owned by Alphabet. Forcing a spin-off of Google Search may not solve any problem that could not be solved in a more direct way. A court would not want to create a remedy that certainly and immediately made a firm much less valuable, harming consumers and labor, on the simple possibility of more competition in the future. One possibility is that, even with all defaults and other restraints removed, 90 percent of consumers who have low switching costs will *still* prefer Google Search.

Interoperability and Portability as Antitrust Remedies

The most successful structural remedy in the history of antitrust enforcement was that of the telephone company in 1982. AT&T had a near monopoly of the U.S. telephone system. At that time, AT&T (the Bell System) was regulated from top to bottom by a combination of the Federal Communications Commission (FCC) and state regulatory agencies. Customers purchased their local and long-distance service and leased their telephone instruments from a single firm. The antitrust litigation against AT&T was brought about by technological changes that were transforming the telephone network from a hard-wired system to one that accommodated significant wireless technology. Along with wireless came the possibility for greater competition.

AT&T's principal antitrust offenses stemmed from its fierce resistance to these changes. It rejected overtures from MCI and Sprint, two wireless providers that wanted to sell telephone service in competition with AT&T but required interconnection with AT&T's network. AT&T had always resisted interconnection and the FCC had gone along. In its 1968 *Carterfone* decision, however, the FCC changed its mind. In the age before cellular phones, Carterfone made an electronic patch that connected citizens' band two-way radios into the AT&T system so that truckers on the road could call home to their families. The FCC held that AT&T had a duty to interconnect. After *Carterfone*, MCI and Sprint pushed aggressive development and litigation strategies to force interconnection. Then the government brought its own antitrust suit against AT&T.

Commercially usable cellular phone technology was just on the horizon, and its success depended on interconnection with the wired network.

AT&T yielded and agreed to a consent decree, which is a negotiated settlement without a trial. AT&T was broken into seven regional Baby Bells. It also divested Western Electric, its subsidiary which made telephone instruments. It retained its "long lines" division, which provided long-distance communications, but this division was now segregated from the local companies. From that point on the telephone instrument market and the long-distance market became competitive, and new firms entered quickly by interconnecting. For local calls, the regional Baby Bells continued to operate in their assigned territories. Their dominance was eroded much more gradually by the entry of cellular communications and also alternative voice transmission technologies. Today even the market for local service is quite competitive.

But another part of the AT&T decree became much more important than the structural breakup. It also provided for mandatory interoperability, or "interconnection." The newly formed Baby Bells were required to interconnect with third parties that wanted to offer telecommunications services on the network. The parties were encouraged to come to interconnection agreements. If they could not, then the regulatory agencies stepped in, taking the claim to arbitration or even to court if necessary. In 1996 this process was merged into the Telecommunications Act, which today compels interconnection "at any technically feasible point" in the network. Under that system both traditional wired and cellular services as well as firms that use other technologies give us both relatively seamless and global interconnection but also competition among more than 850 U.S. telecom service providers. Instruments such as handsets or smartphones are produced and sold competitively. Today you can be in California calling your aunt in North Carolina and the connection is usually so seamless that you cannot even tell who her carrier is or what kind of device she is talking on. That call may pass through several different firms. If you are purchasing wireless service, you have the choice of several, depending on your area, and even more for makers of phones.[8]

When we think about platforms and remedies for monopoly, the AT&T story brings a useful message. A simple injunction may not be adequate for the job at hand. On the other hand, an improperly executed breakup can destroy network effects and make the affected platform much less desirable. But effective interoperability can create the benefits of competition without ruining the network.

The biggest problems facing interoperability remedies are operational. There is no one-size-fits-all fix. Interconnection among firms is actually common, although details vary widely from one situation to another. One omnipresent example is the blanket licensing databases of recorded music, historically run by Broadcast Music (BMI) and the American Association of Composers, Artists, and Publishers (ASCAP). These organizations aggregate nonexclusive licenses for over 16 million songs from owners of copyrights to the digital recordings. They give nonexclusive licenses to commercial licensees, who relicense them to millions of consumers. These intermediate groups include such firms as Spotify, Pandora, Apple Music, Amazon Prime music, the major television and radio networks, Sirius Satellite Radio, and many others. If you subscribe to Spotify or Apple Music you are entitled to a nonexclusive license, which means you can listen to Adele or Mozart as much as you want, but cannot prevent others from listening. Royalties travel from the paying subscriber all the way up the chain to whoever owns the rights to that recording. The entire system effectively provides immediate and legal access to pretty much anything you want to play—and all of this within a system that operates as a market.

A roughly similar system, widely used by academics and researchers, is JSTOR, or Journal Storage. JSTOR.org collects nonexclusive licenses for thousands of articles and other media from roughly 2,000 journals and other digital collections and aggregates them into a database. Subscribers can then access them, acquiring a nonexclusive license to download and use them. Most research libraries and many other institutions are licensees.

Email is another global interoperable network that works so well we rarely think about it. Hundreds of firms offer email services. While interoperability is voluntary, it is key to each provider's success. You can send an email to pretty much anyone you want without concern that they will not receive it. There is a certain amount of standard setting, which governs formatting and protocols for interconnection, but no exclusivity. Anyone who wishes to offer email services can do so, and anyone can use them. Further, consumer access is easy and switching costs are low. In a few minutes' time, someone with internet access can create a free account on gmail.com, yahoo.com, AOL.com, or many others. There are also premium accounts, which cost money but have more features.

Interconnection in markets like email is readily possible because the content is digital and nonrivalrous. These are common but not necessarily universal features of large digital platforms. Some platforms, including Amazon and Uber, sell tactile products such as kitchen toasters or rides. Even here, interoperability is possible although the final product cannot realistically be shared.

A ride-hailing platform could aggregate the services of multiple taxi companies. A larger network could provide both riders and drivers with more options. Depending on how the app is set up, the rider could select a car and the transaction would close. Creating such a system would require some software and operational engineering, but it could make this market more competitive. At least at this writing, Uber has not yet been convicted of any antitrust violation for which such a remedy would be appropriate. Nevertheless, some taxicab companies are voluntarily negotiating driver agreements with Uber, although the agreements apparently will not permit passengers to select a driver. Further, and perhaps problematically, Uber sets the prices.[9] In such a network, with a relatively small number of sellers, the risk of collusion cannot be ignored. A somewhat similar example is flight reservation systems such as Expedia and Orbitz, which give customers immediate and comparative information about carriers and prices for a particular trip. On the demand side anyone can use them, but on the supply side participating airlines are limited. Ticket price fixing is illegal, although immediate and visible reporting of prices encourages parallel price changes.

One way to limit antitrust problems is to make network participation as open on both sides as technical limitations permit. While ASCAP has some 320,000 copyright-holding "sellers," the number of suppliers in the Uber and Expedia situations is much smaller. Further, the dominant air carriers have sometimes excluded low-priced competitors. Collusion and exclusion of discount sellers must both be monitored. Exclusion in such a case is a serious threat because the ability to network creates advantages for its participants. The temptation exists to keep discount competitors off the network. That has been a problem for some local real estate boards. Access to broker-operated multiple listing services may be essential for survival, but some boards have excluded brokers who are willing to accept lower commissions.[10]

Given its substantial promise, when can interoperability be compelled as an antitrust remedy? Answering that is tricky because of the wide variety of technologies and products that digital platforms use. As the AT&T case suggests, dominant firms who already control a network typically do not want to share. On the other hand, non-dominant firms often can survive only by sharing. Further, compelled interoperability will very likely not solve the problem of platforms that handle a great deal of consumer information and could actually make it worse.

Another problem is scope: if interoperability remedies are too broad, they end up homogenizing the participants into a giant single firm. For example, it is difficult to imagine interoperability working among search engines. The likely result would be several firms doing the same thing, essentially combining into a single search engine. By contrast, interoperability succeeded in the telephone system because firms retained most of their business separately. They continue to compete on subscription prices, features, and the sale of devices, but their network is fully interconnected.

As the AT&T decree suggests, antitrust can do some useful things. For example, both Alphabet (Android) and

Apple (iPhone) currently require all platform app sales to be through their individual stores, where they charge large commissions. By contrast, desktop platforms such as Windows create something more akin to a community shopping mall where multiple sellers operate. The owner of the operating system or device does not get a cut of every sale. Apple has so far successfully claimed that this system is too prone to virus or information theft. Beyond that, there is no obvious economic reason that the iPhone and Android platforms should not be opened up to more sellers. Keep in mind that antitrust litigation could force this solution only if the current system was found to be an antitrust violation. Legislation could do it as well.

Related to interoperability is data portability. Simple data portability requires user data to be stored in a common format that customers can transfer, but it need not require ongoing real-time interaction. Built-up data are often a barrier to customer switching. For example, someone who closes out a Facebook account and switches to a different social network site cannot automatically have all of her Facebook history transferred over. This can give more established firms a significant advantage, particularly with respect to long-term users, who have a large history.

A version of this problem appeared in the history of telephone deregulation, where the issue was narrower—namely, phone number portability. Changing carriers is much more costly if you have to change your phone number, which requires informing contacts or losing them, redoing business cards, advertising, and so on. Since the early twenty-first century FCC rules have compelled firms to make numbers "portable," which means that you can keep your number when you switch carriers. The process usually takes a day or two. In addition, both Alphabet and Apple have voluntarily developed programs and procedures for transferring contact lists from one phone system to the other. That considerably lowers the consumer costs of switching.

One question underlying data portability disputes is, who owns your personal information? In ongoing antitrust actions against Facebook, the court agreed with the FTC that user inability to take "photos and associated data/comments with them" operated as a significant barrier to new competition.[11] The court observed that established Facebook users accumulate a valuable (to them) library of information, and that a considerable cost of switching to a different social network was loss of these data. This could be changed with a court-ordered or voluntary provision that gave users control over their data and the ability to transfer their personal library to a different network in a commonly accepted format. An analogous provision in Europe, called the General Data Protection Regulation, attempts to do that.

Data portability in real time might even work as a remedy in the Google Search case. If data scale creates a

One question under-
lying data portability
disputes is, who
owns your personal
information?

significant advantage for the largest search engine, perhaps the database can be licensed out to multiple users who compete by using different search algorithms. For example, thousands of travel agents "share" an electronic database of available airline seats and have the power to book them for customers. While the agents do not control schedules or ticket prices, they do compete on their own fees as well as differing service levels.

One big problem at this stage is that, with the exception of AT&T, we do not have a history of compelled interoperability remedies as we do for more traditional antitrust decrees. Until that happens, interoperability as a remedy will very likely proceed slowly, by trial and painful error.[12]

In one important area the use of antitrust law to encourage interoperability has been disappointing. This is the licensing of standard-essential patents, or SEPs. The problem principally concerns information technology networks such as cellular phone networks, autonomous vehicles, networks that support the sharing of digital images, and the like. To operate on a common network, firms engaged in these systems must be able to share relevant patents. One characteristic of these markets is a very large number of patents, many of which are either difficult to interpret or very weak. Not every device incorporates every patent, and many of the patents may actually not be used at all. Many are invalid. Nevertheless, the cost of litigating

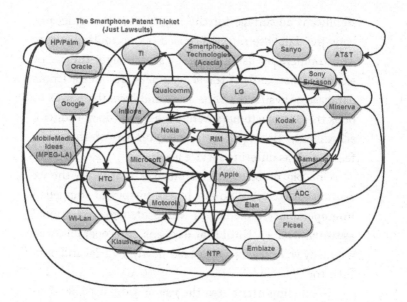

Figure 7

the validity and coverage of every patent in a device such as a smartphone would be prohibitive.

The resulting patent "thicket" for smartphones has been illustrated graphically. This is the complex web of actual patent lawsuits as of 2010 (see figure 7).[13] "FRAND" was created to provide a competitive market clearinghouse for shared technology. The intent was to make cross-licensing of numerous patents in a common technology simpler, and litigation less likely. Firms that agree to participate must declare their relevant patents "standard essential" and then promise to license them to all other participants, including competitors, on "fair, reasonable, and nondiscriminatory," or FRAND, terms.

Two things happen when a patent is declared standard essential. First, it becomes more valuable because it is incorporated into a standard for a shared technology. Firms that build devices can adopt FRAND technology knowing that they will not be guilty of costly patent infringement. As a result, the movement of technology in that area tends to gravitate toward products that are covered by SEPs. Second, however, the owner of the SEP has promised in advance to accept a "fair, reasonable, and nondiscriminatory" royalty, set if need be by an independent court or arbitrator. This outcome reflects a well-known principle: one way to avoid costly and inaccurate government regulation is to invite firms to bid in advance for a position in monopoly markets that have alternative suppliers. For example, if three patented technologies are viable choices for a planned product, their owners can bid against one another for the right to be selected by promising more competitive prices and terms. This system resembles the procedures used by any contractor accepting rival bids from subcontractors for, say, roofing or plumbing. Once a particular firm has made its bid and been selected, however, it may look for ways to cheat after the fact by insisting on a higher price or less competitive terms.

The FRAND system works well if the commitments made by participants are clearly articulated and enforceable. A FRAND violation is a breach of contract. However, if power and anticompetitive effects are present, it can also be an antitrust violation. Here, both the performance of the Justice Department during the Trump administration and the performance of the federal courts have been disappointing. In 2020 the Justice Department split with the FTC, first by issuing a position stating that FRAND violations should not be regarded as antitrust violations. Then it opposed the FTC in a case in which the FTC had quite correctly sued Qualcomm, a dominant maker of modem chips that had violated its FRAND obligations. Qualcomm had refused to license its SEPs to competitors, insisted on above-FRAND royalties, and tried to obtain injunctions against firms that were disputing its terms. The court of appeals sided with the Justice Department and Qualcomm. As a result, the FRAND system has been thrown into some disarray, with less stability in the network and higher prices. Here, antitrust could have played a moderate yet important disciplinary role in managing anticompetitive abuses. Unless the courts change their position, legislation may be the only solution. The alternative is costly licensing battles, inflated royalties, and higher prices.

The policy divide over FRAND reflects an ideological split that runs deep in the patent system. The Trump

Justice Department position reflected a cowboy attitude toward firms in which each one went it alone and stood on its own bottom. That position worked better in old market technologies that do not depend on compatibility or interconnectivity to function. However, if the subject is competitive *networks*, legal rules should help to enable multiple firms to compete on a common network. This necessarily requires a certain amount of cooperation but also ample room for competition in areas where distinctive innovations can succeed. The cellular phone system is a good example of such network design. On the one hand, every firm in the system must meet interoperability and some other compatibility requirements in order to interconnect to the network. On the other hand, these requirements still leave plenty of room for individual service providers and phone manufacturers to compete on price or other features where competition is possible.[14]

Reorganizing Management Instead of Firms

As noted repeatedly in this chapter, one problem with structural remedies is that they can deprive firms of structural efficiency or network effects. In the process they reduce output and harm consumers, labor, and others who benefit from competitive markets. One promising alternative that can make firms more competitive without interfering unnecessarily with their structure is reorganization of management rather than the firm itself.

An important purpose of management reorganization is to change problematic activity from "unilateral" to "collaborative." This may sound like an overly technical distinction, but it actually has important consequences for antitrust policy. The conduct of a single firm is addressed under the very deferential monopolization standards of section 2 of the Sherman Antitrust Act. It cannot be unlawful unless (1) the firm is a "monopolist," with a market share typically exceeding 60 percent or so, and (2) the conduct excludes rivals from the market in an unreasonable way. By contrast, the conduct of a group of actors operating by agreement is addressed as a restraint of trade under section 1 of the Sherman Act. The market share requirements are substantially lower, typically 30 percent or so, and the conduct need not be exclusionary. For example, price fixing and market division can both be illegal even when they do not exclude. Further, hard-core offenses such as price fixing can be condemned under the per se rule, which requires no proof of market power. The differences are dramatic in one important area—namely, the law of refusal to deal with competitors. As noted previously, under U.S. law a firm acting on its own has almost no antitrust duty to deal with its rivals. By contrast, concerted refusals to deal get much more aggressive treatment, including per se condemnation of naked boycotts.

These same distinctions apply when a group of firms with independent business interests collaborate in a common enterprise. Important Supreme Court cases involving the Chicago Board of Trade, the Associated Press, and the NFL addressed such ventures, as well as lower court cases involving hospitals and real estate boards. In the Supreme Court's *Associated Press* case, for example, several newspapers had joined together to create an incorporated wire service that enabled them to share news stories, thereby eliminating the need for a newspaper to have a reporter in every city.[15] But AP had a restrictive membership policy that generally denied membership to a newspaper if another member newspaper in the same town objected. The Supreme Court condemned the restriction and then ordered the AP members to deal with nonmembers in a nondiscriminatory fashion. Under today's law that could not happen if AP was a unitary firm, which is generally free to refuse to deal with competitors. The court was willing to create that remedy only after concluding that AP should be treated as an agreement among multiple competing participants.

In the Supreme Court's *American Needle* decision in 2010, the individual NFL Football teams were members of a single incorporated association that licensed out the teams' separate trademarks.[16] The court held that the association's decision not to license to the plaintiff should be treated as the collaborative action of the individual teams, not as unilateral action. That could spell the difference between liability and nonliability.

What the courts have not yet done is require reorganization of a single firm's management structure so as to makes its actions collaborative rather than unilateral. Such remedies have some practical advantages. Mainly, the court need not interfere in the structure of the firm or the extent of its network effects. It could retain its efficient size and scope. The network itself would remain unitary, but the number and variety of managing decisionmakers would increase so as to include active participants in the industry with their own separate businesses. In that case the heightened standards of section 1 of the Sherman Act could be brought to bear. For example, the telephone system is a single unitary network whose various pieces are owned and operated by numerous firms delivering wired and wireless services, instruments, and network infrastructure. Anecdotally, price fixing has not been more common in that industry than in others, but it is clearly reachable should it occur.

One way to conceptualize this is to think about a firm such as Amazon as a shopping mall of individually owned stores rather than a single department store. The single store selects its products and makes all the important decisions about product selection, display, and pricing unilaterally. By contrast, in a large shopping mall dozens of different store owners share a building, very likely a parking lot, and some common needs, such as security and management. But each merchant owns or leases its own store, and price fixing among them is just as unlawful as it is out there in the wider market. If two or more stores agreed to exclude a certain manufacturer, that could be reachable as well.

Rather than breaking up a firm such as Amazon or Alphabet, market decisions about sales, purchases, pricing, and the like could be assigned to a diverse board of those who have their own business dealings with that firm. For example, if a board of Amazon's active merchants, suppliers, customers, and other involved parties had the authority to make Amazon's pricing selection, display, and other commercial decisions, the board members would be subject to the more aggressive standards of section 1 of the Sherman Act. That could make sales on the Amazon platform more competitive without ruining the economies of scale or network effects that have benefited both the firms and their consumers. Further, their diversity would make them more inclined to compete with one another rather than collude.

Conclusion

Three rules should guide the formation of effective antitrust remedies against big tech: *first*, understand the

Three rules should guide the formation of effective antitrust remedies against big tech: (1) understand the problem; (2) do something that is reasonably calculated to fix it; and (3) do no (unnecessary) harm.

problem; *second*, do something that is reasonably calculated to fix it; and *third*, do no (unnecessary) harm. Unfortunately, while those rules can be stated in a couple of lines, their statement belies the great complexity and difficulty that courts have encountered in creating suitable remedies for big tech antitrust violations. Nevertheless, adhering to them is essential to an effective antitrust policy. By focusing on appropriate goals we should be able to develop some common ground for assessing the formidable problems—as well as unprecedented benefits—that big tech presents.

Breakup
The divestment of a firm, by court order, whereby the firm sells off one or more of its subsidiaries, branches, or productive assets, thus breaking the firm into at least two parts.

Cartel
Association of two or more competing firms that agree to cooperate on market output, price, or territories without integrating their production or distribution.

Clayton Antitrust Act
The second major U.S. antitrust law, passed in 1914, which prohibits a form of price discrimination, anticompetitive tying and exclusive dealing, and anti-competitive mergers. It also contains a first attempt to immunize labor from the antitrust laws.

Competition
A state of affairs in which each firm's pricing decisions are significantly limited by the output and pricing of other firms. Under perfect competition, no firm can profitably charge more than its marginal cost; price is minimized consistent with profitability, and output is maximized. As a market becomes more competitive, the competition benefits consumers with lower prices and workers with more jobs.

Data portability
A practice under which data are stored in a format that can be readily transferred and shared with others, generally on demand of its owner.

Digital
Technically, a technology that stores and processes data in binary form, usually represented by 0s and 1s. In law and business, it refers to digital product output, which can include text, graphical images, music, video content, and operational code.

Digital firm
A business firm that either creates digital content or contains a significant component of digital content in its production or distribution.

Dominant firm
A firm that is very large in relation to its market, although not necessarily the only one. Antitrust law generally identifies dominant firms based on a market share exceeding 50 percent or 60 percent.

Exclusive dealing
A situation in which, by agreement, typically between a supplier and a dealer, the dealer will sell the supplier's product exclusively. For example, a Ford automobile dealer may agree that the only new cars it sells will be Fords.

Horizontal agreement
An agreement between two or more competitors or with potential competitors to restrict competition among them or to facilitate joint production or development.

Injunction
A court order that prohibits a firm from doing something ("prohibitory injunction") or that requires a firm to do something ("mandatory injunction").

Intellectual property (IP) rights
Patents, copyrights, trademarks, or trade secrets that give to their owners a right to prevent duplication or copying of the features covered by the IP right.

Interoperability
A characteristic of a product or system that allows it to work with other products of systems. For example, two firms may share current operational information and procedures, enabling users to interact with one another, typically on a network.

Marginal cost
The increased cost a firm incurs when it produces one additional unit. Under perfect competition, a firm's prices are driven down by rivals to its marginal cost, but sales at a price lower than marginal cost are usually irrational.

Market power
The power of a single firm or a group (cartel) to profit by reducing output and raising price above the competitive level; relatedly, the power of a firm or group to exclude rivals while maintaining prices above the competitive level.

Merger
A transaction in which one firm acquires all or a substantial interest in the stock or productive assets of another firm.

Monopoly
In economics, a firm that controls 100 percent of the market for a certain product; in law, a firm with a very large market share of a certain product, typically exceeding 60 percent. An economist would describe this as a "dominant firm."

Most favored nation (MFN) clause
A clause in a sales or licensing contract promising that one party's deal will be at least as favorable as the deal offered to any other party.

Network
A market organization in which multiple firms or persons combine or interconnect production, development, or distribution in order to deliver a more desirable product.

Nonrivalous good
A good such as a patent or copyright that can be used by one person without diminishing the amount that is left over for others.

Oligopoly
A state in which only a small number of competitors operate in a market, enabling the firms to maintain prices above costs without an explicit contract or agreement.

Potential competition merger
A firm's acquisition of another firm that is not an actual competitor but that realistically threatens to become one.

Predatory pricing
Charging a price below one's costs in order to drive rivals out of business, and then recoup costs by charging monopoly prices thereafter.

Product differentiation
Distinction between products that compete with one another in the same market but have somewhat different characteristics; a marketing strategy. Such firms typically compete on the basis of quality or features in addition to price. Automobiles, cellular phones, and digital games are good examples.

Public domain
The intellectual property space in which inventions or ideas are not protected by an IP right, or to which such rights have expired, making them freely available to the public to copy or use.

Relevant market
A grouping of products that resemble one another sufficiently that those inside the market can be said to compete, while those outside the market do not compete with those inside.

Robinson-Patman Act
Antitrust legislation, passed in 1936, that sometimes makes it unlawful to sell to two dealers at different prices such that the dealer who pays the higher price is injured.

Self-preferencing
A situation in which a multibrand seller gives its own products or brands preferential treatment over those of others.

Sherman Antitrust Act
The United States' first antitrust law, passed in 1890, which prohibits agreements "in restraint of trade" and "monopolization."

Tech firm
A firm for which a major component of *production* is digital technology. Today virtually every firm is a consumer of digital technology. A tech firm's products need not be purely digital, but a significant portion of its production or distribution must be.

Technological tie ("tech tie")
The linking of two or more products by technological design rather than by contract, such that the products must be used together. For example, the Apple iPhone is designed to work only with the iOS operating system.

Trust
An early form of business organization based on a common law "trust" agreement that permitted multiple corporations to be joined together and operated as one.

Two-sided platform (two-sided market)
An entity that intermediates between two (or more) groups of users. For example, Uber does not sell rides but rather arranges rides between drivers and passengers. Another example is a magazine that balances its revenue between paying subscribers and advertisers.

Tying arrangement
An agreement whereby a seller sells one product only on the condition that the buyer take a second product as well, such as a requirement that those purchasing a seller's computer operating system must also take its internet browser.

Vertical agreement
An agreement between two or more firms that ordinarily stand in a buyer-seller relationship, such as a manufacturer and its suppliers or its dealers.

Vertical merger
The acquisition by one firm of a vertically related firm, normally either a seller or a buyer.

Preface

1. Market share numbers in this book are mainly from statcounter.com, which is free to use and calculates real-time usage shares for various digital products. The assumptions about market definition that Statcounter uses are not necessarily the ones that would be used in antitrust litigation.

2. *NCAA v. Alston*, 141 S.Ct. 2141 (2021).

3. Erik Hovenkamp, "Platform Antitrust," *Journal of Corporation Law* 44 (2019): 713, https://papers.ssrn.com/sol3/papers.cfm?abstract_id=3219396.

Chapter 1

1. Frank Norris, *The Octopus: A Story of California* (New York: Doubleday, Page and Co., 1901); Ida M. Tarbell, *The History of the Standard Oil Company* (New York: McClure, Phillips and Co., 1904), 182; Udo Keppler, "Next!" (cartoon), *Puck*, September 7, 1904, https://www.theodorerooseveltcenter.org/Research/Digital-Library/Record?libID=o277854.

2. *Henry v. A.B. Dick Co.*, 224 U.S. 1 (1912).

3. See the FTC's website at https://www.FTC.gov.

4. *Hoover v. Ronwin*, 466 U.S. 558 (1984).

5. *North Carolina Dental Examiners v. FTC*, 574 U.S. 494 (2015).

6. *Motion Picture Patents Co. v. Universal Film*, 243 U.S. 502 (1917). For a good history, see Alexandra Gil, "Breaking the Studios: Antitrust and the Motion Picture Industry," *NYU Journal of Law & Liberty* 3 (2008) 83, http://www.law.nyu.edu/sites/default/files/ECM_PRO_060965.pdf.

7. Herbert Hovenkamp, "Can the Robinson-Patman Act Be Salvaged?," Promarket, October 13, 2022, https://www.promarket.org/2022/10/13/can-the-robinson-patman-act-be-salvaged.

8. See Herbert Hovenkamp, *Principles of Antitrust*, 2nd ed. (St. Paul: West Academic, 2021), chap. 12.

9. Herbert Hovenkamp, "The Invention of Antitrust," *Southern California Law Review* 96 (2022) 131, https://papers.ssrn.com/sol3/papers.cfm?abstract_id=3995502.

10. Herbert Hovenkamp and Fiona M. Scott Morton, "Framing the Chicago School of Antitrust Analysis," *University of Pennsylvania Law Review* 168 (2020), 1843, https://papers.ssrn.com/sol3/papers.cfm?abstract_id=3481388.

11. For a good summary, see Nicole Callan, Leon Greenfield, and Perry Lange, "Antitrust Populism and the Consumer Welfare Standard: What Are We Actually Debating?," *Antitrust Law Journal* 83 (2020) 293, https://www.jdsupra.com/post/contentViewerEmbed.aspx?fid=185249f0-6146-4598-b7f4-7efd0f27e5a9.

12. See Herbert Hovenkamp, "Are Monopolists or Cartels the True Source of Anticompetitive US Political Power?," Promarket, August 3, 2022, https://www.promarket.org/2022/08/03/are-monopolists-or-cartels-the-true-source-of-anticompetitive-us-political-power.

13. *U.S. v. Alcoa, 148 F.2d 416, 430* (2d Cir. 1945).

14. Herbert Hovenkamp, "The Slogans and Goals of Antitrust Law," *NYU Journal of Legislation & Public Policy* 25 (2023): 705, https://papers.ssrn.com/sol3/papers.cfm?abstract_id=4121866.

Chapter 2

1. *U.S. v. Continental Can Co.*, 378 U.S. 441 (1964); *U.S. v. DuPont*, 351 U.S. 377 (1956); *U.S. v. Microsoft*, 253 F.3d 34 (D.C.Cir. 2001); *FTC v. Facebook*, 581 F. Supp. 3d 34 (D.D.C. 2022).

2. *Philadelphia Taxi Assn. v. Uber*, 886 F.3d 332 (3d Cir. 2018).

3. Daniel A. Crane, "Market Power without Market Definition," *Notre Dame Law Review* 90 (2014): 31.

4. *Kodak v. Image Technical Services*, 504 U.S. 451 (1992).

5. Richard Gilbert, *Innovation Matters: Competition Policy for the High-Technology Economy* (Cambridge, MA: MIT Press, 2020).

6. Gilbert, *Innovation Matters*.

7. Herbert Hovenkamp, "Are Monopolists or Cartels the True Source of Anticompetitive US Political Power?," Promarket, August 3, 2022, https://www.promarket.org/2022/08/03/are-monopolists-or-cartels-the-true-source-of-anticompetitive-us-political-power.

8. National Grocers Association, "Independent Grocers Respond to Biden Antitrust Executive Order," July 9, 2021, https://www.nationalgrocers.org/news/16341.

9. *N.C. State Board of Dental Examiners v. FTC.*, 574 U.S. 494 (2015).

10. *Brown Shoe Co. v. U.S.*, 370 U.S. 294, 320–324 (1962).

11. Robert H. Bork, *The Antitrust Paradox: A Policy at War with Itself* (New York: Basic Books, 1978), 107.

12. United States Department of Justice and Federal Trade Commission, 2023 Draft Merger Guidelines, https://www.justice.gov/atr/2023-merger-guidelines.

13. On litigated win rates, see Jason Rantanen, Charles Neff, Eweosa Owenaze, and Alison Williamson, "Who Appeals (and Wins) Patent Infringement Cases?," *Houston Law Review* 60, no. 289 (2022), https://houstonlawreview.org/article/66211-who-appeals-and-wins-patent-infringement-cases.

14. *Chicago Board of Trade v. U.S.*, 246 U.S. 231 (1918).

15. Herbert Hovenkamp, "The Antitrust Text," *Indiana Law Journal* (forthcoming), https://papers.ssrn.com/sol3/papers.cfm?abstract_id=4277914.

16. *Epic Games, Inc. v. Apple, Inc.*, 67 F.4th 946 (9th Cir. 2023).

17. See Richard H. Thaler, *Misbehaving: The Making of Behavioral Economics* (New York: Norton, 2015).

18. David S. Evans, "The Economics of Attention Markets" (SSRN), abstr. 3044858, April 2020, https://papers.ssrn.com/sol3/papers.cfm?abstract_id=3044858.

19. See OECD, *Rethinking Antitrust Tools for Multi-Sided Platforms* (OECD, 2018), https://www.sipotra.it/old/wp-content/uploads/2018/07/Rethinking-Antitrust-Tools-for-Multi-Sided-Platforms-2018.pdf.

Chapter 3

1. *Brunswick Corp. v. Pueblo Bowl-O-Mat, Inc.*, 429 U.S. 477 (1977).

2. *Aspen Skiing co. v. Aspen Highlands Skiing Corp.*, 472 U.S. 585 (1985); *Verizon Communications, Inc. v. Trinko*, 540 U.S. 398 (2004).

3. Harrity LLP, "Patent 300," 2023, https://harrityllp.com/patent300 (based on 2022 figures).

4. Michal Addady, "Merchants Say Amazon Is Copying Their Products," *Fortune*, April 20, 2016, https://fortune.com/2016/04/20/amazon-copies-merchants.

5. E.g., *Bonito Boats v. Thunder Craft*, 489 U.S. 141 (1989) (invalidating state statute that created IP-like protection for boat hull that federal patent law did not protect).

6. *FTC v. Actavis, Inc.*, 570 U.S. 136 (2013).

7. *Fashion Originators Guild v. FTC*, 312 U.S. 457 (1941).

8. James Bessen, *The New Goliaths: How Corporations Use Software to Dominate Industries, Kill Innovation and Undermine Regulation* (New Haven, CT: Yale University Press, 2022).

9. *Google LLC v. Oracle Am., Inc.* 141 S. Ct. 1183 (2021).

10. John Latchem, "Packaged-Media Retail Trends Marked by Shrinking Shelf Space, Short Supplies," Media Player News, November 4, 2021, https://www.mediaplaynews.com/packaged-media-retail-trends-marked-by-shrinking-shelf-space-short-supplies.

11. Anthony Dean, "What's the Future of DVDs and Blu-Rays?," Diverse Tech Geek, October 12, 2021 (last update August 5, 2022), https://www.diver setechgeek.com/whats-future-dvds-blu-rays.

12. Rob Errera, "Printed Books vs eBooks Statistics, Trends and Facts [2023]," Toner Buzz, 2023, https://www.tonerbuzz.com/blog/paper-books-vs-ebooks -statistics (last visited April 26, 2023).

13. *Tops Markets, Inc. v. Quality Markets, Inc.*, 142 F.3d 90, 99 (2d Cir. 1998).

14. *Epic Games, Inc. v. Apple, Inc.*, 67 F.4th 946 (9th Cir. 2023).

15. See Erik N. Hovenkamp, "Restraints on Platform Differentiation," *Yale Journal of Law and Technology* 25 (2023): 271, https://papers.ssrn.com/sol3 /papers.cfm?abstract_id=4164172.

16. *Jefferson Parish Hospital District v. Hyde*, 466 U.S. 2 (1984).

17. For a good contextual analysis, see Randal C. Picker, "The Arc of Monopoly: A Case Study in Computing," *University of Chicago Law Review* 87 (2020), 523, https://chicagounbound.uchicago.edu/uclrev/vol87/iss2/9.

18. *BMI, Inc. v. Moor-Law, Inc.*, 527 F.Supp. 758 (D.Del. 1981), aff'd, 691 F.2d 490 (3d Cir. 1982).

19. *Standard Oil Co. of California et al. v. U.S.*, 337 U.S. 293, 305 (1949).

20. *CalComp, Inc. v. IBM*, 613 F.2d 727 (9th Cir. 1979).

21. Erik Hovenkamp and Kevin Bryan, "Startup Acquisitions, Error Costs, and Antitrust Policy," *University of Chicago Law Review* 87 (2020), 331, https:// chicagounbound.uchicago.edu/uclrev/vol87/iss2/3.

22. Herbert Hovenkamp, "Antitrust and Platform Monopoly," *Yale Law Journal* 130 (2021), 1952, 2045.

Chapter 4

1. *U.S. v. Microsoft Corp.*, 253 F.3d 34, 103 (D.C. Cir. 2001).

2. These issues are developed more fully in Herbert Hovenkamp, "Antitrust Harm and Causation," *Washington University Law Review* 99 (2021) 787.

3. The principal government case against Microsoft is *U.S. v. Microsoft Corp.*, 253 F.3d 34 (D.C. Cir. 2001). The principal private case is *Kloth v. Microsoft Corp.*, 444 F.3d 312 (4th Cir. 2006).

4. See Herbert Hovenkamp, "Antitrust and Platform Monopoly," *Yale Law Journal* 130 (2021) 1952, https://papers.ssrn.com/sol3/papers.cfm?abstract _id=3639142.

5. *Apple, Inc. v. Pepper*, 139 S.Ct. 1514 (2019).

6. *Standard Oil Co. v. U.S.*, 221 U.S. 1 (1911). See U.S. Government, Federal Trade Commission, *Report on the Price of Gasoline in 1915*, April 11, 1917.

7. The story is recounted in *Verizon Communications, Inc. v. Law Offices of Curtis V. Trinko*, 540 U.S. 398 (2004).

8. See Herbert Hovenkamp, "Antitrust Interoperability Remedies," *Columbia Law Review Forum* 123 (2023), 1, https://papers.ssrn.com/sol3/papers.cfm ?abstract_id=4035879.

9. Hovenkamp, "Antitrust Interoperability Remedies."

10. E.g., *U.S. v. Realty Multi-List, Inc.*, 629 F.2d 1351 (5th Cir. 1980).

11. *FTC v. Facebook, Inc.*, 581 F.Supp.3d 34, 51 (D.D.C. 2022).

12. See Fiona M. Scott Morton and Michael Kades, "Interoperability as a Competition Remedy for Digital Networks" (SSRN), abstr. 3808372, March 19, 2021, https://papers.ssrn.com/sol3/papers.cfm?abstract_id=3808372.

13. Mike Masnick, "Meet the Patent Thicket: Who's Suing Who for Smartphone Patents," Techdirt, October 8, 2010, https://www.techdirt.com/2010 /10/08/meet-the-patent-thicket-who-s-suing-who-for-smartphone-patents.

14. Herbert Hovenkamp, "FRAND and Antitrust," *Cornell Law Review* 105 (2020), 1683, https://papers.ssrn.com/sol3/papers.cfm?abstract_id=3420925.

15. *Associated Press v. U.S.*, 326 U.S. 1 (1945).

16. *American Needle, Inc. v. NFL*, 560 U.S. 183 (2010).

FURTHER READING

Listings preceded by an * appear with a link where they are available online at no charge. Some may require users to register.

Bessen, James. *The New Goliaths: How Corporations Use Software to Dominate Industries, Kill Innovation, and Undermine Regulation*. New Haven, CT: Yale University Press, 2022.

*Bryan, Kevin, and Erik Hovenkamp. "Startup Acquisitions, Error Costs, and Antitrust Policy." *University of Chicago Law Review* 87 (2019): 331, https://papers.ssrn.com/sol3/papers.cfm?abstract_id=3376966.

Gavil, Andrew I., and Harry First. *The Microsoft Antitrust Cases: Competition Policy for the Twenty-first Century*. Cambridge, MA: MIT Press 2014.

Gilbert, Richard J. *Innovation Matters: Competition Policy for the High-Technology Economy*. Cambridge, MA: MIT Press, 2022.

*Hovenkamp, Erik. "The Antitrust Duty to Deal in the Age of Big Tech." *Yale Law Journal* 131 (2022): 1483, https://papers.ssrn.com/sol3/papers.cfm?abstract_id=3889774.

*Hovenkamp, Herbert. "Antitrust and Platform Monopoly." *Yale Law Journal* 130 (2021): 1952, https://papers.ssrn.com/sol3/papers.cfm?abstract_id=3639142.

*Hovenkamp, Herbert. "The Invention of Antitrust," *Southern California Law Review* 96 (2022): 131, https://papers.ssrn.com/sol3/papers.cfm?abstract_id=3995502.

Hovenkamp, Herbert. *Principles of Antitrust*, 2nd ed. St. Paul: West Academic, 2021.

*Kovacic, William E. "The Chicago Obsession in the Interpretation of US Antitrust History." *University of Chicago Law Review* 87 (2020): 459, https://lawreview.uchicago.edu/publication/chicago-obsession-interpretation-us-antitrust-history.

*Lemley, Mark A., and Robin Feldman. "Atomistic Antitrust." *William and Mary Law Review* 63 (2022): 1869, https://papers.ssrn.com/sol3/papers.cfm?abstract_id=3793809.

*Morton, Fiona Scott, Gregory S. Crawford, Jacques Crémer, David Dinielli, Amelia Fletcher, Paul Heidhues, and Monika Schnitzer, "Equitable Interoperability: The 'Super Tool' of Digital Platform Governance," *Yale Journal of Regulation* 40, no. 1013 (2023), https://papers.ssrn.com/sol3/papers.cfm?abstract_id=3923602.

*Salop, Steven C. "What Is the Real and Proper Antitrust Welfare Standard? Answer: The True Consumer Welfare Standard." *Loyola Consumer Law Review* 22 (2010): 336, https://lawecommons.luc.edu/lclr/vol22/iss3/3.

*Shapiro, Carl. "Antitrust in a Time of Populism," *International Journal of Industrial Organization* 61 (2018): 714, https://papers.ssrn.com/sol3/papers.cfm?abstract_id=3058345.

Viscusi, W. Kip, Joseph E. Harrington Jr., and David E. M. Sappington. *Economics of Regulation and Antitrust*, 5th ed. Cambridge, MA: MIT Press, 2018.

HERBERT HOVENKAMP is the James G. Dinan University Professor, University of Pennsylvania Carey Law School and the Wharton School. He is a Fellow of the American Academy of Arts and Sciences, and in 2008 won the Justice Department's John Sherman Award for lifetime contributions to antitrust law. His writing includes *The Opening of American Law, 1870–1970*; *Enterprise and American Law, 1836–1937*; *Antitrust Law* (with the late Phillip E. Areeda and the late Donald F. Turner); and *Federal Antitrust Policy: The Law of Competition and Its Practice*; *IP and Antitrust* (with Mark D. Janis, Mark A. Lemley, Christopher Leslie, and Michael Carrier). He lives with his partner in Haverford, Pennsylvania, and has two adult sons.